Naszej Najukoc...

...krysia

Londyn Lipiec 1989

ANTIQUE SPOONS

ANTIQUE SPOONS
A Collector's Guide

Victor Houart

SOUVENIR PRESS

First published 1982 by Souvenir Press Ltd,
43 Great Russell Street, London WC1B 3PA
and simultaneously in Canada

Book designed by Pamela Mara

ISBN 0 285 62499 7

Filmset and printed in Great Britain by
BAS Printers Limited, Over Wallop, Hampshire

CONTENTS

ACKNOWLEDGEMENTS

I wish to thank the following persons who very kindly helped with information or illustrations for this book and among them Mr Eric J. G. Smith, Department of silver, Phillips, London; Mr S. E. F. Beechey, Assay Master, Birmingham Assay Office, who went out of his way to help; Mr George R. Dalgleish, research assistant, National Museum of Antiquities of Scotland, Edinburgh; Miss S. M. Hare, librarian of the Worshipful Company of Goldsmiths, London; Mr J. den Hertog, of the Rijksmuseum voor Volkskunde, Het Nederlands Openluchtmuseum, Arnhem; Mrs Jorunn Foosberg, Head Curator of the Norsk Folkemuseum, in Oslo; Mr Derrick Jenkins, of the Welsh Folk Museum, Cardiff; Mrs M. Raissac, curator of the Musée Bouilhet-Christofle, in Paris; Mr L. Carrier, curator of "les Musées d'Orbigny-Bernon et des Beaux Arts," La Rochelle; Mr Yves Solier, curator of the Musée Archéologique, Narbonne; Dr. H. Lanz, director of the Historisches Museum, Basel; Mrs Eleanor Thompson, of the silver department, Sotheby Parke Bernet & Co, London; Prof. Marcel Massart, for decyphering Greek inscriptions on spoons, and Mrs De Coninck, department of silver, Musées Royaux d'Art et d'Histoire, Brussels.

Brussels, 1st January 1982.

1 SPOONS OF THE ANCIENT WORLD

~~~~~~

The spoon may not be as old as the world but, as a humorist once said, it is at least as old as soup, which goes back a long way. Whatever the date of its invention thousands of years ago, the spoon is without doubt the oldest table utensil of all, used to drink and to eat right from its beginnings.

It is not necessary to go as far back as the Garden of Eden, but in the neolithic period, between 5000 and 2500 years BC, before any type of metal had been forged, primitive men were making clay spoons and bone scoops, using any suitably hollowed item to hold liquid, any suitable shaped shells to do duty as spoons. Stone spoons have survived from the Upper Pleistocene epoch, which overlaps the beginning of the Stone Age. Wooden spoons were made very early; a good example, dating from the period 3000–2500 BC, was found in excavations carried out in the region of Lucerne, Switzerland, and is now in the Landsmuseum in Zurich.

Such spoons have been found in many places in Europe, including England of course, notably one found in Hassocks, Sussex. Scoops made of bronze were produced in the Bronze Age which followed the neolithic period, and metal spoons have continued to be made ever since, side by side with the wooden spoons which have been used universally down to the present time. Bronze spoons of Celtic origin, dating back to the Bronze Age, have also been found in various places. It should be noted that what the prehistorians call bronze does not correspond to the definition found in modern dictionaries; the word itself was unknown until the fifteenth century, and the name did not appear in print before the middle of the sixteenth. The bronze we know today is an alloy of copper and tin, but prehistorians apply the term to all alloys of a whitish or yellowish colour which contain some copper.

The Egyptians made elegantly shaped metal spoons, quite small,

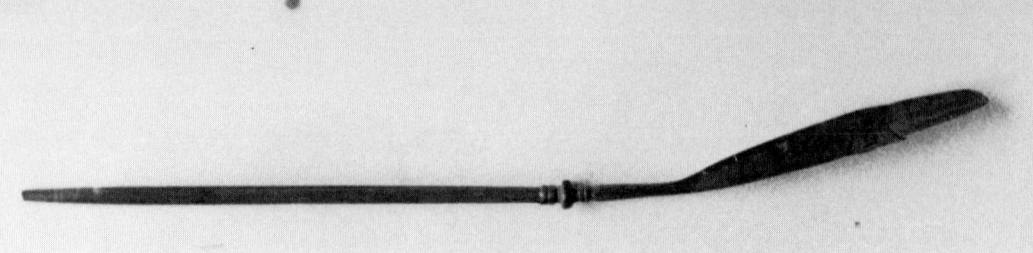

with a spike at the end of the stem, perhaps to eat solids, meat or fish, perhaps to extract snails or shellfish from their shells. This type of spoon was taken up first by the Greeks, then by the Romans, who made great quantities of them in bronze and in silver. The Egyptians also used a kind of silver toilet spoon, very fancy, examples of which have been found in tomb excavations. These spoons, whose origin goes back many centuries BC, must have been used to mix all kinds of ingredients with water or other liquids, but of course it is difficult to tell. Their stems are ornate and of great variety, while their bowls, very charming, are engraved with scenes. The Louvre Museum in Paris has some of these treasures in the Clot-Bey collection, but it is unlikely that others will appear on the market. Some are engraved with scenes such as a beautiful girl playing the lute among lotus flowers, a young man cutting the same lotus flowers, a dog with a shell in its mouth.

The Greeks and then the Romans used spoons of various designs, including those known as the *cochlear* and the *ligula* the latter apparently the real ancestor of our present-day spoons. Incidentally, the French word for spoon, *cuiller*, comes from the word cochlear, which is the Greek name for a type of seashell similar to a snail shell. It has of course nothing to do with the fact that men have used seashells as spoons from the beginning of time.

There has always been controversy about the kind of ladle which the Greeks called *cyathus* and the Romans *simpulum*. Both are in the form of a small vase to which a stem has been attached. Most historians in France believe that they were in fact ladles used to take wine out of wine jars, the amphoras. They may have been used to serve wine at table. This type of ladle is often represented on Greek and Roman vases decorated with everyday scenes. It appears that the Greek cyathus was more elegant than its Roman counterpart, the bowl being shallow, with a stem curving at its extremity to take the form of an animal's head. The Louvre Museum has a magnificent

10

cyathus with two heads of snakes at the end of the stem. Another one, discovered in Arles, has a duck's head at the end of its stem. The Roman simpulum originally took the shape of a small porringer to which a stem had been attached. The rough shape of the early simpulum was improved as time went by; instead of being rounded the bowl became ovoid, and the straight stem became more elegant and slightly curved. It seems that the Latins adopted the cyathus of the Greeks and used it to serve liquids at the table, the word simpulum referring only to the ladle used in various religious ceremonies. If the Greek cyathus appears often on Greek earthenware vases of long ago, the simpulum of the Romans is also represented on sculptures, even pieces of money. Many varieties of these ladles are known, the bowls sometimes having the shape of a small cylinder, quite deep.

The cyathus even became a legal measure in Greece and Rome, although nobody knows its exact capacity. The Romans used the cyathus to measure solids in the form of dried matters, powders, etc. It seems that the cyathus must have represented about one ounce. Below it there was the 'ligula', representing half a cyathus, and finally the 'cochlear', a quarter of a cyathus. These various spoons, or ladles, were not used to take liquids to the mouth, but to serve liquids or powders.

The Greeks and Romans used two types of spoons, the cochlear and the ligula, which were measures, but were also used to eat at

Two Roman bronze ligula spoons with pear-shaped bowls. The bottom spoon has a knop at the end of its stem which at one time must have been pointed like a diamond knop. *Museum of Art and History, Brussels*

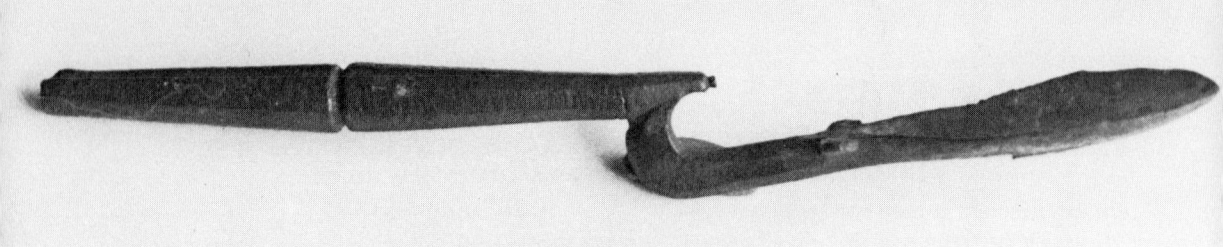

A Roman ligula spoon in bronze, found in a river where it had probably spent the last 2000 years.

table. They are well represented in practically all the important museums. The cochlear was a copy, more or less, of a more ancient Egyptian spoon. The original model had a very tiny circular bowl and a narrow straight stem of rounded section, ending, like its Egyptian model, in a spike. It was rather small, with a diameter rarely exceeding 1 cm, and an average stem length of about 5 cm. The name suggests that the cochlear must have been intended for eating certain types of shellfish, using the spiked end to extract the fish from its shell, although probably it was also used to pick up other types of food like meat, or to pierce eggshells. Later the Romans slightly improved the shape of their cochlears, and the bowl became elongated, with the stem attached to it by means of a tiny disc called the 'elbow' of the spoon. This second type of cochlear is also well represented in the museums, and now and then one appears in salesrooms.

The great majority of these spoons were made in the metal called bronze by archaeologists, and many were made out of silver. Many such spoons have been discovered during excavations—for instance in the ruins of Pompeii—together with the ligula, the real ancestor of our modern spoon. The ligula spoon had a narrow stem of rounded section attached to an elongated bowl by means of a rat-tail, a system of attachment which was taken up again in Europe in the Seventeenth and Eighteenth centuries. The stems of the known ligulas are not always straight—some may be slightly curved—and instead of ending in a spike they very often had an ornament as finial. Some were profusely decorated, and some ligulas found in Pompeii even had three pearls in a row at the end of their stems.

There seems to have been no attempt in ancient times to differentiate between ligula and cochlear, and Daremberg and Saglio point out in their *Dictionary of Greek and Roman Antiquities* that contemporary authors employed the words indiscriminately.

12

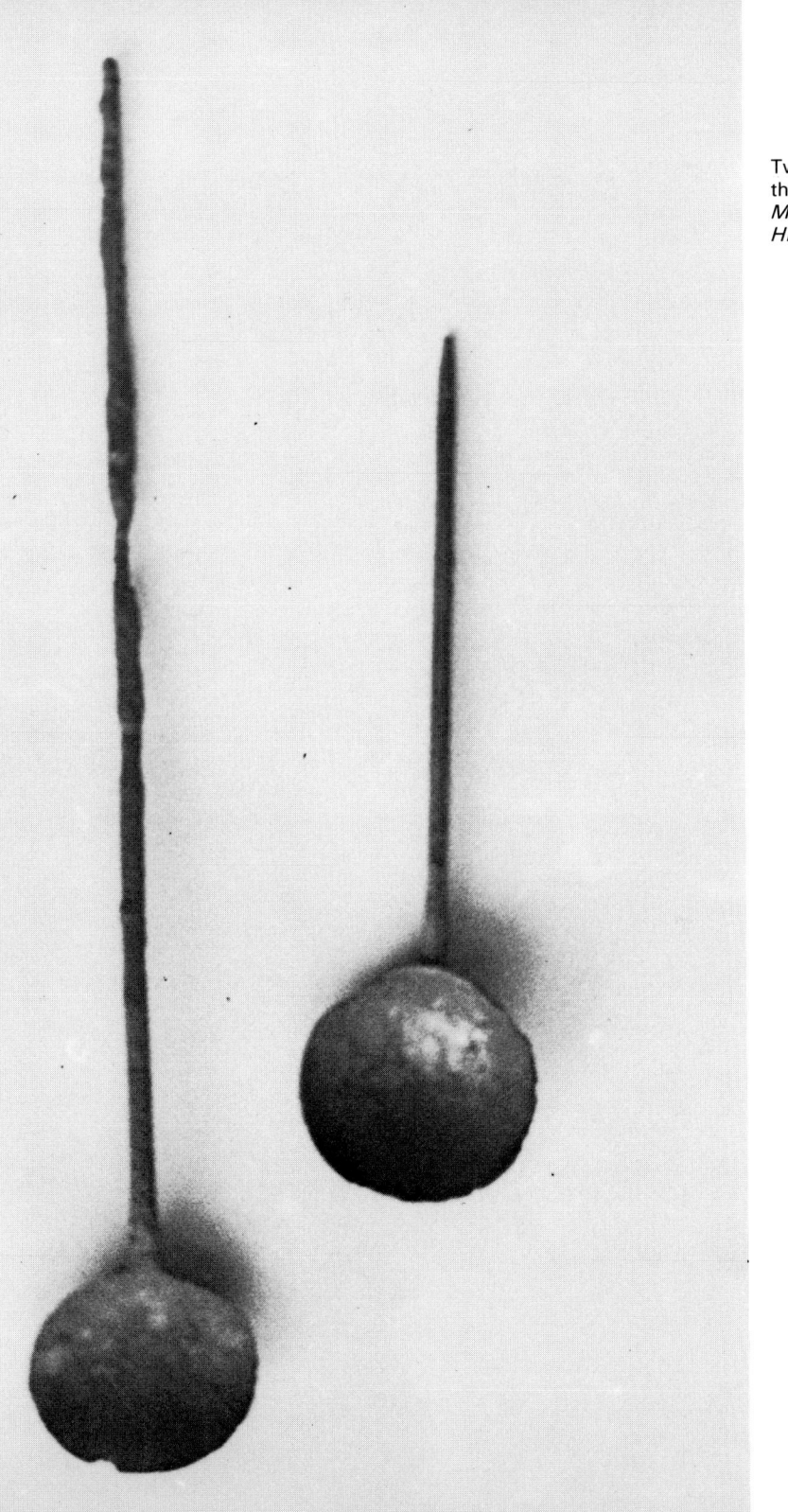

Two Roman spoons of
the cochlear type.
*Museum of Art and
History, Brussels*

An early Roman ligula spoon, which, seen from above, shows that it is the real ancestor of our modern spoons. *Museum of Art and History, Brussels*

According to modern usage, the ligula was used at the table, to eat, and the cochlear was used as a measure of capacity. Doctors used it to measure their medicines, liquids and powders, and the wise Isidore, bishop of Seville at the beginning of the Seventh century AD, when the Roman Empire had already completely collapsed, could mention that the smallest type of measure was still the cochlear, worth half of a drachma.

As well as the cochlear and ligula, there was another, much rarer, type of spoon which was made by the Greeks and the Romans but has no particular name. It was probably used to take ointments from narrow-necked jars, and has a long stem of square or rounded section and a bowl very similar to that of a narrow spoon, rectangular, about 3 cm long and 1 cm in width.

To sum up, we can say that, as a rule, the cochlear was smaller than the ligula and its stem always ended in a spike, while the stem of the ligula ended in an ornament. The bowl of the cochlear, very small, was originally circular but slowly became elongated, sometimes reaching a perfect oval. The ligula, used to eat at table, had an elongated bowl right from the beginning. The two types were generally made of bronze, more occasionally of silver, and some bone ones have been found.

These spoons from the ancient world, Egyptian, Greek or Roman, are not easily come by, most of them having been discovered in excavations and from there found their way to museums. They do appear on the art market, but very rarely.

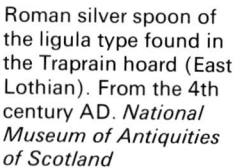

Roman silver spoon of the ligula type found in the Traprain hoard (East Lothian). From the 4th century AD. *National Museum of Antiquities of Scotland*

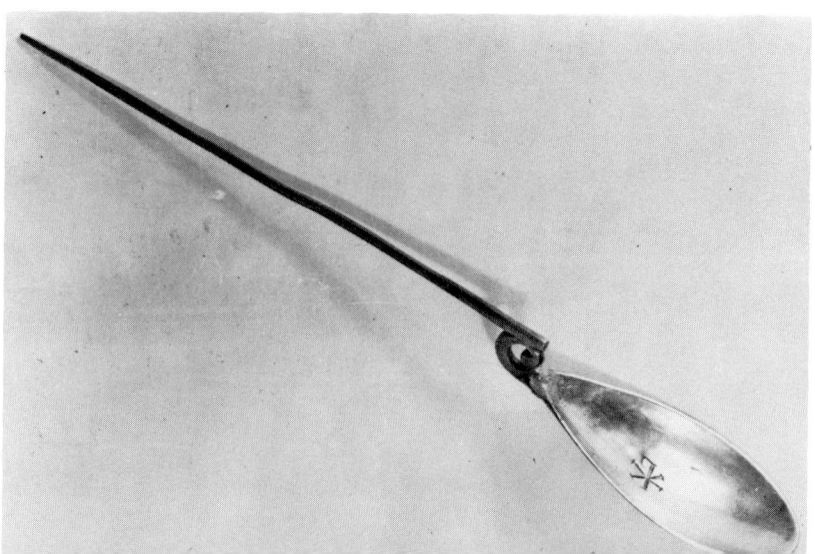

2 SPOONS OF THE LATER ROMAN EMPIRE

The later Roman Empire covers a period which stretched from the early third century AD until about the fifth century, starting in fact when the old western Roman Empire was beginning to crumble and the Barbarians were poised on the frontier. But the influence of Rome did not cease suddenly around the year 500 AD, which marks the end of the Roman Empire. Many characteristics of the Roman world persisted in western Europe a long time after the historical collapse.

Between the third and seventh centuries AD, some beautiful spoons were produced, mostly in silver but also in bronze, with a great variety of stems: tapering, octagonal in section, rising at the end into a spatula; tapering and fluted, octagonal section terminating in a conical knop; tapering, rounded in section; square in section near the bowl, the remainder round in section with a number of parallel lines at each end; first hexagonal near the bowl, then round in section. The bowls of these marvellous Roman (or so-called Roman) spoons were of all shapes already—pear or egg-shaped, circular, fiddle-shaped or nearly, narrow shovel-shaped—which goes to show that nothing was invented by later western European craftsmen, who most likely got their inspiration from the Roman models.

All these spoons, most of them engraved with mottoes, names, or lines from well-known Greek writers, are called 'Later Roman Empire spoons' by the archaeologists, although quite a lot of those surviving were made when the Roman Empire, even the later one, was only a memory. Maybe they should be called early Christian or even Byzantine, for some were found in the region of the eastern Mediterranean, but in fact they have been found everywhere, in Greece, France, Germany, Italy, Cyprus and other countries. Some are typically Christian in their decoration and inscriptions, others

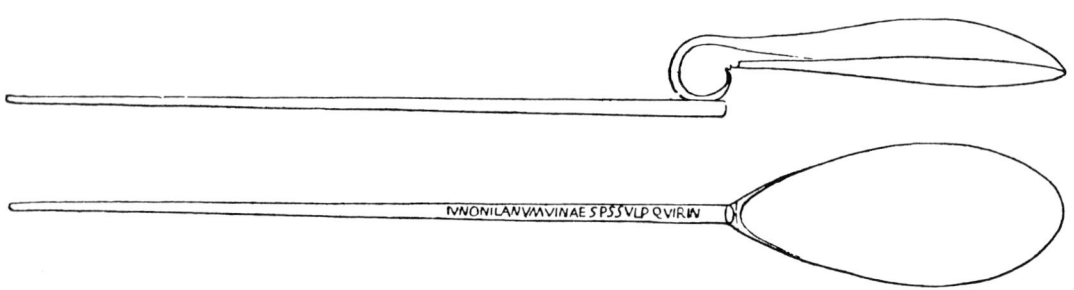

Typical silver spoon of the later Roman Empire, with pear-shaped bowl and tapering hand of octagonal section. *From the Catalogue of Early Christian Antiquities by O. M. Dalton, London 1901.*

are typically pagan, but they all have great elegance and would grace any collection.

Wherever they come from, these Later Roman Empire spoons are beautifully decorated, and engraved with figures and lettering inside the bowl or on the reverse. Monograms or mysterious marks appear sometimes on the circular joint, the shoulder, between bowl and stem. Many of them bear the chrism, the monogram composed of the letters X and P, which did not appear before the end of the third century AD and is found on many buildings, on coins and all kinds of other objects. (Another early Christian sign found on some silver spoons is an engraved fish.) The chrism monogram was invented by the Christians living in Rome, and the famous letters X and P are the two first letters of the name of Christ written in Greek, 'Xpictos' (Christos, as it should be pronounced). The sign appears on many spoons which were probably given by one Christian to another.

Such spoons are mentioned in many documents of the period, including the 'Life of St Augustine' by his biographer Possidius,

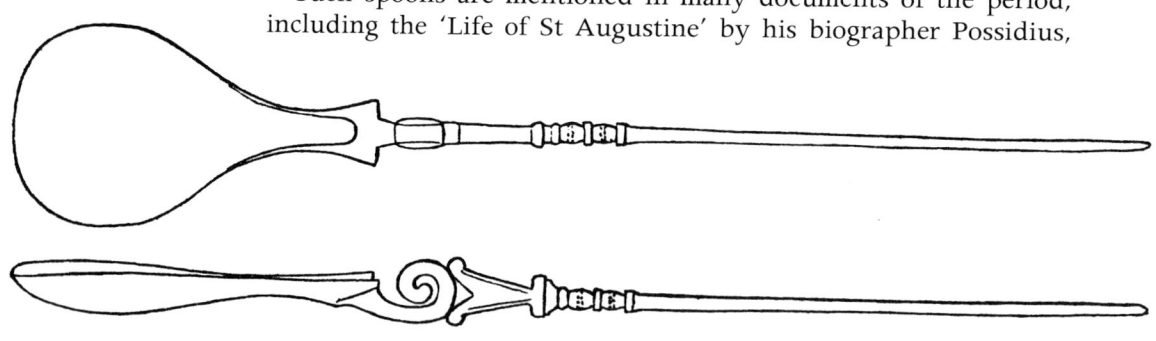

Late Roman Empire silver spoon with a fiddle shaped bowl and another type of attachment. *From the Catalogue of Early Christian Antiquities by O. M. Dalton, London 1901.*

who writes about the saint 'using only silver spoons'. In their 'Dictionary of Christian Archaeology and Liturgy', published in 1914, Dom Fernand and Dom Henri Leclercq mention many other saints who had a love for silver spoons, such as St Rémy, who in his last will left 'three other silver spoons marked with my name'.

Spoons of the period were very often inscribed with the owner's name, the names of apostles or venerated saints, and mottoes and wishes. Some bear the words '*Potens Viva*' (Sovereign, living), some '*Venerias vivas*' (Enjoy the pleasures of love), a sentence far from being early Christian. Other inscriptions are '*Utere felix*' (Use me with happiness) and '*Victura Vivas*' (Live to conquer). The museum of Smyrna, in Turkey, has a spoon of the cochlear type, 25 cm long,

Examples of decoration appearing on the disc joining bowl to stem of some later Roman Empire silver spoons, now in the British Museum, London. These designs were most often nielloed and represented various monograms, sometimes using a latin cross or formal flowers as here. *From the Catalogue of Early Christian Antiquities by O. M. Dalton, London 1901.*

with the engraving: '*Balnea Vina Venus Faciunt properantia Fata*' (Baths, wines and love accelerate the destiny). Some are inscribed with wishes such as '*Bene vivas*' (Live well). Some others are only engraved with the names of the owners or, rarely, with the name of the silversmith. Some have inscriptions in Latin and Greek, like the Smyrna spoon mentioned above. The shoulder (disc) of the spoon is inscribed with a monogram and a Latin cross, but its stem bears the inscription, in Greek: 'When you sacrifice watch your hernia'.

Most of these interesting later Roman Empire spoons have been found in excavations, and Cabrol and Leclercq mention one treasure discovered in 1792 in Aquilee, on the island of Grado, off the Venetian coast. Aquilee, a very important harbour at the end of the Roman Empire, was completely destroyed by Attila the Hun in 452 AD

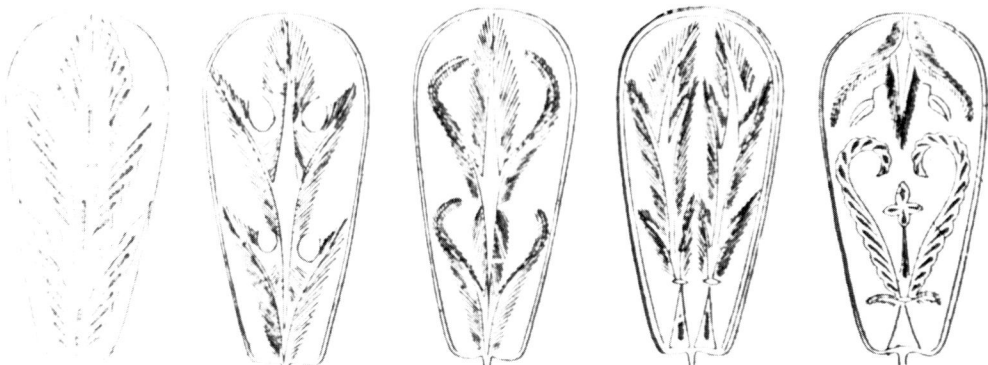

Designs found on the bowl reverse of silver spoons from the late Roman Empire, from the Cyprus Treasure, now in the British Museum, London. *From the Catalogue of Early Christian Antiquities by O. M. Dalton, London, 1901*

and today it is completely abandoned. Six silver spoons of the fourth century had been buried with a child, and probably belonged to him. The two bigger spoons had their oval bowls engraved with figures of his family and with the motto: '*Eusebiorum dignitas*' (The honour of the Eusebii). The four smaller ones, two with oval bowls, the others respectively egg and pear-shaped, were engraved with scenes from the sacrifice of Abraham, the Adoration of the Magi, and the christening of a child. Their present whereabouts are unknown.

Another hoard reported by Cabrol and Leclercq in their monumental work was found in Porto, not far from Rome. Of the nine spoons unearthed, one is supposed to be in the Vatican, seven in the Naples Museum, in the Castelloni collection. The last was supposed to be in England at the end of the nineteenth century, in a collection in Wiltshire, and is described as having the engraving of a peacock in niello on the inside of the bowl. Two were without inscriptions, three decorated with crosses, letters and numbers. The remaining three were engraved with the names Alexander, Faustus and Quadragesima, each preceded by a cross and followed by Roman cyphers. These are presumably the owners, unless of course they were the silversmiths' names.

But the best place to study the Later Roman Empire or early Christian spoons is the British Museum in London, which houses the

18

spoons found in four different discovered treasures or hoards, respectively on the Esquiline Hill near Rome, on the hill of St Louis in Carthagus, on the north coast of Cyprus, and at Lampsacus, near the Black Sea.

All the beautiful spoons discovered in these four hoards, together with many other silver objects, are described by O. M. Dalton in the British Museum catalogue of *Early Christian Antiquities*, published in 1901. In the Esquiline hoard are examples of pear-shaped, oval and mandolin-shaped bowl types. Of two spoons with stems of octagonal section, one terminates in a conical knop, another expands

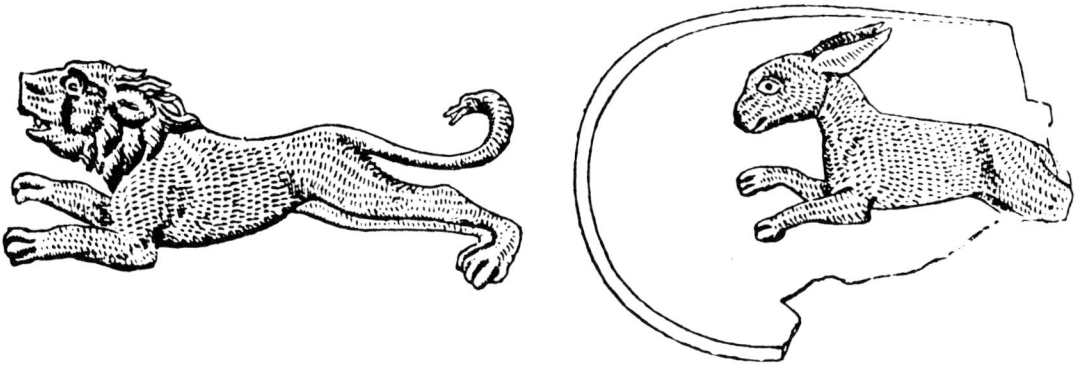

Examples of engravings found in late Roman Empire silver spoons of the Cyprus Treasure, now in the British Museum, London. *From the Catalogue of Early Christian Antiquities, by O. M. Dalton, London, 1901*

to a spatula engraved with simple geometrical designs. Only one has a shallow circular bowl. These spoons, discovered as early as 1793, date from the fourth to the fifth century.

Twelve spoons in silver were discovered during excavations carried out in Carthagus. They belong to the same period as the Esquiline spoons, and seven of them are of particular interest as they differ somewhat from the usual Roman types. The spoons have a deep circular bowl and a short stem of octagonal section terminating in a knop. The square panel at the joint of the bowl and stem is decorated with the usual Latin cross between two scrolls, in niello.

19

One of the spoons, with a pear-shaped bowl whose reverse represents a leaf, has the sacred monogram XP engraved inside the bowl.

The dozen spoons discovered in Lampsacus all date from the sixth and seventh century. Most of them are inscribed with names or mottoes in Greek, difficult to translate. Five of them, with pear-shaped bowls, are engraved in Greek with the names of the apostles, Matthew, Peter, James, Mark and Luke. According to Dalton, the names were probably in niello. One of these magnificent spoons is engraved with a sentence in Latin, taken from Virgil and not that Christian either: 'Omnia vincit amor et nos cedamos amori' which means 'Love conquers everything and we submit to love'.

It is the Cyprus hoard, now in the British Museum, that contains the most magnificent spoons from the Later Roman Empire. They all date from the sixth century AD, and appear to be more Byzantine than Roman. The hoard included twenty-five spoons, among other treasures. Most of them may be called typically Roman, having pear-shaped bowls with shoulders in the shape of a disc, and straight stems. One spoon has a stem of hexagonal section with the remainder of round section, the two parts being separated by a short baluster. But the most astonishing and best-known spoons in the collection are a set of eleven. Unusually big (they measure 26 cm), their baluster stems are terminated by a small knop. The spoons have no shoulder at all, and the stems are attached directly to the elongated bowls, which are decorated in relief with various animals including a tiger, boar, horse, stag, lion, bull, griffon, ram and hare.

The British Museum also contains other Later Roman Empire spoons found in various places such as Augsburg, Rome, Metz, and even in the River Seine, in Paris. They are of the usual construction, with pear-shaped bowls terminating in a vertical disc connecting stem to bowl, some of the discs decorated with the usual Latin cross in niello. It is curious to think that the spoonmakers of the Later Roman Empire and even a bit later never thought of adding small figures at the end of their spoon stems. It was so common, for instance, for them to decorate their silver pins with tiny figures of Venus in various poses.

These Later Roman Empire spoons are often a delight to look at. Unfortunately they are difficult to come by.

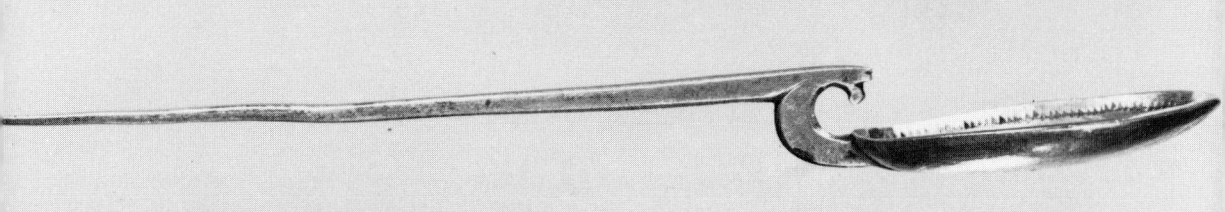

Two views of a late Roman silver spoon of the cochlear type, now in the Historisches Museum, Basel.

Another spoon of the later Roman Empire, the 'dolphin spoon', found in The Traprain hoard (East Lothian), with a deep and rounded bowl. It has a very short stem known as a 'fist stem'. Late 14th century. *National Museum of Antiquities of Scotland*

3 SPOONS OF THE EARLY MIDDLE AGES

It is difficult, in fact practically impossible, for a collector to discover spoons made during the period of the early civilizations, the Later Roman Empire and the Byzantine Empire. (This latter term is used for convenience only, as most of the still extant spoons from the fifth to seventh centuries were not made in Byzantium itself.) Very ancient spoons in silver or bronze can be found in great numbers in many museums, but they seldom appear in sales rooms or in antique shops. The same applies to mediaeval spoons made before the end of the fourteenth century. They are rarely on the market, and because most of them are not marked, it is difficult to assign a definite period, and even less an approximate date.

Early mediaeval spoons are rare for one simple reason: not many were produced. Spoons in silver, bronze, latten, rock crystal or semi-precious stones were only made for a selected few—the rich noblemen and members of the clergy. The vast majority of people living in those socially dark ages used spoons made out of various woods. Some spoons of the period are of a simple type: circular bowls, straight stems with the end cut at right-angles, made of silver, bronze, pewter or brass. Other spoons were more elaborate: again a circular bowl with a straight stem, long or very short, the top decorated with a figure—a saint, the Virgin Mary, or other figures. Some were made of rock crystal or semi-precious stones. Then there were folding spoons, practically always in silver, the first appearing during the later fourteenth century. One mysterious kind of spoon was made of silver or bronze, with the figure of an animal's hoof on top of the stem. This type was probably introduced to Western Europe by returning crusaders.

Mediaeval spoons are of course the direct descendants of the Roman spoons of the ligula type, but whereas Roman and Byzantine spoon-makers had already been producing all types of bowls centuries before, the craftsmen of the High Middle Ages always made theirs circular until the end of the thirteenth century. We know very little about the spoons produced before the twelfth century, as they are rarely mentioned in contemporary texts. That they did of course exist is proved by the few extant examples in museums, for instance the ninth-century Saxon spoon, with double bowl, in the British Museum, supposed to be the oldest extant English spoon. Spoons from the so-called Dark Ages are sometimes represented in miniatures decorating manuscripts from the ninth century, or carved on bas-reliefs from the twelfth century. Some of these spoons, of the serving type, can be seen on the capitals which ornament stone columns in the cathedral of Vézelay, in France.

It seems that the first table spoons of the Middle Ages, which appeared in the twelfth century, had a length of about 18 cm, with shallow circular bowls and stems of square or hexagonal section, the end cut at right-angles or terminating in a diamond-shaped finial, at least in France (the motif appears later in Britain). The British Museum has a collection of five spoons with diamond-shaped finials which were found in the wall of St Michael's Church, Abberley, Worcestershire, in 1963 and are attributed to the end of the fourteenth century. It is also during the twelfth century that another type of spoon appears for the first time. This type still has a shallow circular bowl, but on a very short stem. On the Continent it is known in Dutch as a 'vuistlepel' in French as a 'cuiller de poing', both names means 'fist spoon'. These short-stemmed spoons kept being made until well into the sixteenth century.

Some 'fist spoons' dating from the twelfth century had their bowls connected to the stems by means of a lion's head, or sometimes a dragon's head. This style was still in use in the fifteenth century,

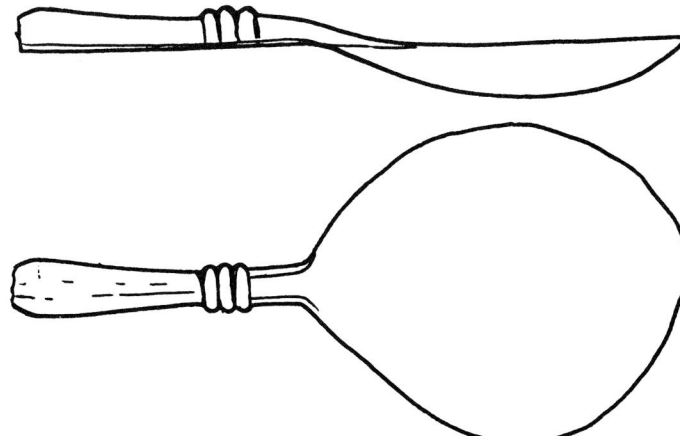

Bronze spoon of the early Middle Ages. This type of spoon with a very short stem, known on the continent as a 'fist spoon', has been made for many centuries.

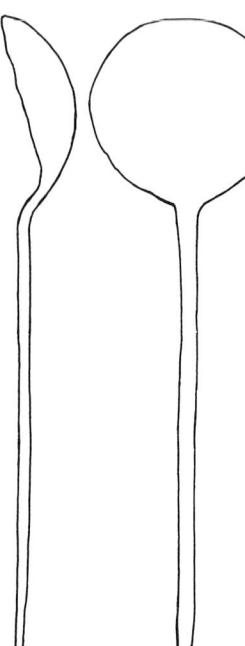

A typical bronze spoon with cut stem end and rounded bowl of the Early Middle Ages.

even to attach seashell bowls to their silver stems. It is only at the end of the thirteenth century that spoon bowls started being not only elongated, becoming gradually pear or fig-shaped, but also deeper. At the same time the spoons themselves became much smaller— between 13 and 15 cm in length. It seems logical to think that the spoons with shallow circular bowls were made to eat all kinds of solid foods, such as stews for instance, and that the new type of spoon with the deeper, elongated bowl was made to eat liquid food such as soups.

If it is certain that the spoons with cut ends and diamond-shaped finials are among the oldest, nobody has ever been able to fully explain the form and function of the hoof spoon, a type which is found as late as the eighteenth century, but also in the Middle Ages. The Brussels Museum of Art and History has two of those spoons. They are made of bronze, and were discovered with other spoons with cut ends in excavations carried out in Bavay (France), together with a set of Roman spoons of the cochlear type. Their stems terminate in the shape of a hoof, probably a horse's, but since the bowl is pear-shaped they can only be attributed to the fourteenth century, unless of course they are much older. The British Museum has two little hoof spoons made of silver, the stems terminating in a goat's hoof. Like the Brussels spoons, their stems are slightly curved. The British Museum spoons were discovered at Cyzicus, in Asia Minor, and are probably of great antiquity. The controversy as to where the hoof spoon originated is far from being settled. Those of great antiquity, like the Brussels and British Museum examples, are rare. The very name is mentioned for the first time in England during the sixteenth century.

Starting in the seventeenth century, and for reasons unknown, the production of hoof spoons seems to have increased, so that examples can be found in quite a lot of places. The Mayer van den Berg Museum, in Antwerp, has a silver spoon of the type, with an oval bowl and a curved stem attached to the bowl by a rat-tail. Made in Antwerp in 1628–9, it is 17 cm long. But hoof spoons were not only made of bronze or silver. The van Beuningen Museum, in Rotterdam, has two such spoons in pewter, one of them attributed to the first half of the seventeenth century, the other, shorter, one to the eighteenth century. The first has a twisted spiral stem, which is

24

rather unusual. Two other hoof spoons are in a private Belgian collection. Although made in the seventeenth century, they are in bronze with egg-shaped bowls and square-section curved stems. But whatever the place and period of origin of the extant hoof spoons, they always have a curved stem, and usually a fig- or pear-shaped bowl, except in Britain, where they often have a leaf-shaped bowl. These spoons are a real problem. Why the animal hoofs? Why the curved stems? Why were they made until the eighteenth century? The animal hoofs might have had a symbolic meaning at the beginning, but it seems to escape everybody nowadays. Those very ancient and strange spoons would grace any collection today.

It is at the end of the thirteenth century that the stems of spoons become somewhat shorter and the bowl elongated. The stems become even shorter as a rule during the fourteenth century, their normal length being a mere 13 cm. Spoons, as a matter of fact, are very rarely mentioned in documents of the twelfth century, and serious references to them in contemporary texts start in the early thirteenth century. From that period onwards, spoons start being mentioned more and more often in wills and inventories of rich households, although the descriptions are not always as complete as one might wish.

Of course the mediaeval clerks who wrote down lists of household belongings were not experts or collectors, and they only gave the briefest descriptions. So brief, in fact, that it is sometimes practically impossible to determine the type of spoon referred to. On the other hand, some of the descriptions given are so complete that there can be no doubt about the types of spoon described, and the information so conveyed is of the highest interest to modern collectors. In many cases even the shortest mention gives a clue to where and when a certain type of spoon started being made for the first time. Such documentary references to spoons are found not only in Britain but everywhere else—in France, Italy, Germany and many other countries—for the spoon is a universal utensil. In this way we learn that spoons were made during the early Middle Ages, before the end of the fourteenth century, from all kinds of woods, such as boxwood, juniper wood, poplar wood and all the various kinds of fruit wood. They were also made in gold, silver, brass, bronze, latten rock crystal, serpentine, cornelian, mother-of-pearl and seashell.

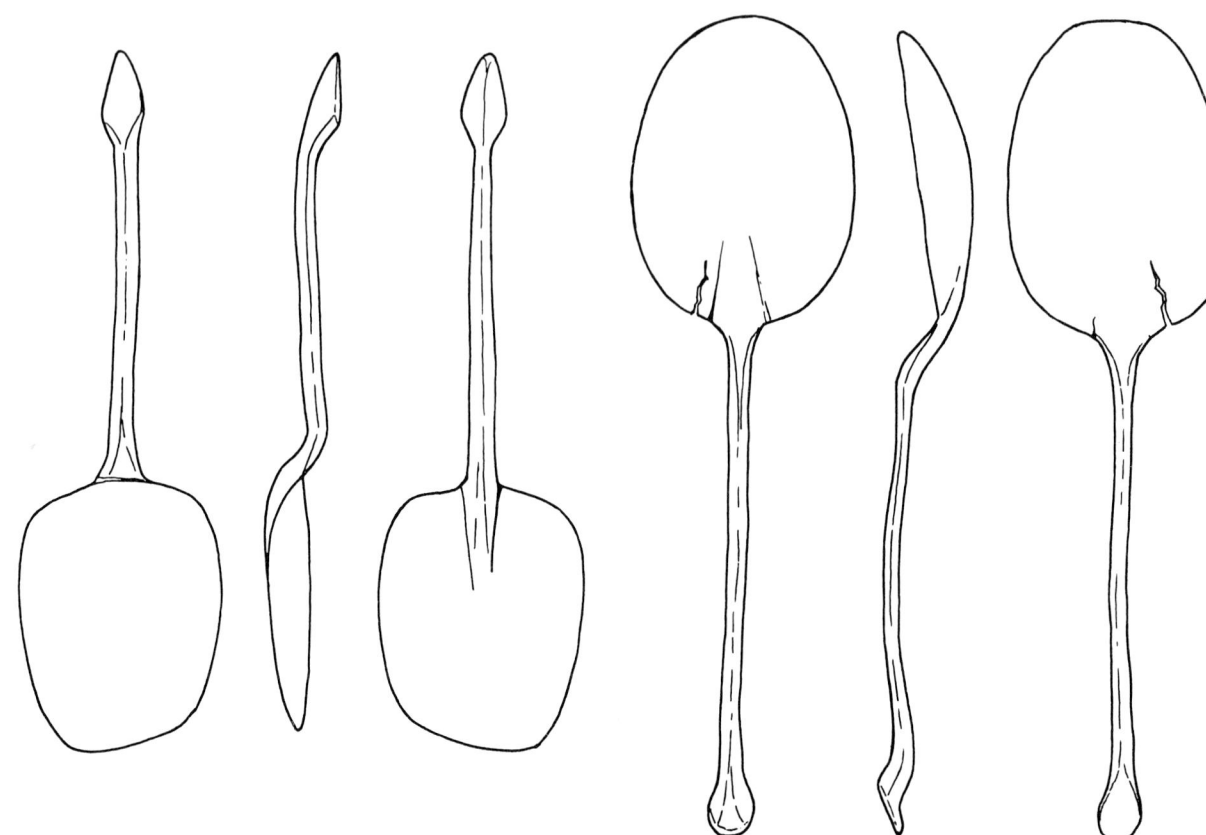

Drawing of two bronze hoofspoons from the early Middle Ages, with square section stem, a net tail, and near end bowl. Probably 13th century.

Unfortunately, all wooden spoons from the Middle Ages have disappeared, and the examples still extant belong mainly to the sixteenth century.

In his *Dictionary of Furniture and Decoration*, Henri Harvard mentions many French inventories which give a clue to certain still unrecorded spoons. An inventory dated 1269, that of the earl of Nevers, mentions '*quatre cuillers à drageoirs en argent*' (four sweet-box spoons, in silver). This poses a problem. For we know very well what a 'dragée' is now—a sweet consisting of an almond covered with coloured sugar. The type of spoon is mentioned continually from the thirteenth until the sixteenth century. A document entitled 'Silverware claimed by the Crown from the heirs of Louis I d'Anjou', and dated 1385, refers to '*un drageoir en argent blanc aux armes de la Royne et une cuiller à espicier*' (a sweet-box in white silver with the Queen's arms and a spice spoon). Did the spoon belong to the sweet-box? Those French 'dragcoirs' so commonly mentioned may also have been receptacles for the spices which were so rare in the Middle Ages, for spice spoons are also often mentioned. In the inventory of the French crown jewels, drawn up in 1418 and quoted by Henri Harvard, there are *'deux cuillers d'argent à prendre epices'* (two silver spoons for taking up spices). Some French authors believe that these 'drageoir spoons' were in fact used to take up spices and even jam. It is very likely that we will never know for sure what those spoons were used for or what they looked like, for in a hundred documents they are mentioned but never described.

But at least we can be sure that silver and gold spoons were made as early as the thirteenth century. One of the first mentions appears in the inventory of Clemence of Hungary, dated 1328: 'a dozen spoons in silver and two spoons and one fork in gold'. The same inventory also mentions that she had 'four little spoons in crystal', which is how we know that spoons in rock crystal started being made at least as early as the thirteenth century. Many other spoons in rock crystal are mentioned in documents of the fourteenth century, and they were still being produced in the sixteenth century, mainly in Germany. Gold spoons, so rare in museums, were made at a very early date too, for they are mentioned in countless documents. In the inventory of the possessions of Louis of Anjou, in 1368, are 'six spoons in gold' and 'a spoon in gold with a sapphire on top of the stem'. Louis of Anjou was even more blessed than Clemence of Hungary, for he also had 'a silver spoon, with the reverse of the bowl decorated with his own coat of arms'. As far as can be determined this is the first known mention of an armorial spoon.

But besides silver, gold and armorial spoons, others of even greater splendour were made during the fourteenth century. Take for instance the inventory of a rich French nobleman, Etienne de la Fontaine. In 1351 he paid a French goldsmith 'to make and forge a spoon in gold, the stem of which is decorated with armorial fleurs de lys and fleurs de lys after nature, enamelled in blue and light red, with a castle at the end of the stem'. This document, reported by Victor Gay, is proof that such heavily decorated spoons, with a figure or arnament as finial, must have been produced at least during the first half of the fourteenth century. Here the finial is a tiny castle in gold, but it is most likely that other figures were used all through the century to decorate what were called *'cuillers à ymaiges'* — picture spoons. In fact the inventory of Louis of Anjou, already mentioned, states that besides his armorial spoon the nobleman also owned eleven other silver spoons, four of them plain, the rest with ornaments or precious stones at the end of the stems. It is regrettable that once again the clerk neglected to describe the ornaments.

The inventory of Charles V of France, dated 1380, indicates still another type of spoon which originated during the fourteenth century. At his death, the king had *'une cuiller à un gland au bout et fut à la reine Jehanne de Bourbon'* (an acorn spoon which belonged to Queen Jehanne of Bourbon). This establishes that acorn spoons were being made as early as the fourteenth century, and in fact other French documents suggest that they were quite popular at the time. Again the inventory of Valentine of Milan, written in Latin in 1389 and reported by Victor Gay, mentions '36 spoons in silver gilt with an acorn on top of the stems'. And in an English will dated 1351, reported by Michael Clayton, a certain John de Holeigh bequeathed a collection of 'twelve spoons with skernes' (acorns).

Clearly acorn spoons were popular, probably from the first half of the fourteenth century, practically everywhere in Europe. However, the Victoria and Albert Museum, in London, has in its collection two spoons from the island of Cyprus, which have a fig-shaped bowl and a diamond-section stem with an acorn on top of the stem. They are attributed to the thirteenth century. So it seems that acorn spoons were not a western European invention, but that they originated somewhere in south-east Europe at an earlier date. It can only be assumed that they reached western Europe by way of Venice. They remained popular for a long time, and some were still being made at the end of the seventeenth century.

The inventory of King Charles V of France, written just after his death in 1380, reveals yet another type of spoon. The text is quite explicit: 'two spoons in gold, one small, one big, one of which is a feeding spoon' (*'cuiller à biberon'*). There is no doubt that what we have here is a spoon with a spout, made to feed infants or sick persons. The French term *biberon* is still used today to designate a child's feeding bottle. Once again, it is regrettable that the clerk who wrote down the will did not give a detailed description of the spoon in question. Certain French authors of the nineteenth century, like Victor Gay, believe that the so-called *cuiller à biberon* was used to pour sauces at the king's table. That is a possibility, but it does not explain why the fourteenth century clerk should have used the word *biberon*. In all likelihood the Charles V spoon was in fact a feeding spoon, and probably not the first of its kind. This spoon of 1380 must have looked like some still extant examples of the sixteenth century, which have a bowl shaped like a circular scoop, with a spout on one side and a short curved handle. The spoon must be the ancestor of the English feeding spoon which appeared at the end of the seventeenth century.

Another rare spoon which appeared for the first time during the fourteenth century, but which could have been made even earlier, is the so-called folding spoon, the oldest example of which seems to be the silver one presently in the Rheinisches Museum, in Cologne, and dated 1329, although there is one in the Scarborough Museum which is supposed to date from about 1300. The folding spoon is just a normal spoon with a hinged stem allowing the owner to fold it in two. It was very useful during the Middle Ages, and even for a long time after, as people had to carry their own spoons if they intended to eat outside their own houses, and this type took up less room in your pocket.

Many of these interesting spoons were made all over Europe during the fourteenth century and until the end of the seventeenth century. Their existence in the fourteenth century is confirmed by many contemporary texts. The will of a certain Pierre Forget of France, written in 1394, contains the entry: 'one spoon in silver, folding'. Victor Gay reports folding spoons in the French royal accounts of 1398, where it is stated that the king was the owner of 'three little spoons in enamelled silver, with hinges, each hanging from a little chain, to be used in the king's sauce-room'. Such folding spoons are very rare it appears in English silver, and most extant examples are of the late seventeenth century. They are found more often on the Continent, where spoon collectors are much rarer than ancient spoons. But even on the Continent, it is very rare to find a folding spoon made before the sixteenth century.

The Coventry Maidenhead spoon, from about the middle of the 14th century. *Victoria and Albert Museum, London*

A last type of spoon which appeared during the fourteenth century, but may have existed already in the previous century, is the armorial spoon engraved inside the bowl or on its reverse with the coat of arms of its owner. We have seen that Louis of Anjou had one in 1385. The inventory of King Charles VI of France, written in 1399, mentions '*une cuiller à un manche tuers, à 2 pommeaulx émaillés aux armes de la reine Jehanne de Bourbon*' (one spoon with a twisted stem, with two pommels enamelled with the coat of arms of Queen Jehanne of Bourbon). A pommel is normally the small ball which crowns the handle of a sword or a dagger, but this royal spoon has two pommels, and presumably they were placed one on top of the other at the top of the stem. References to two pommels on spoons are reported elsewhere in the fourteenth century, as in the inventory of Charles V of France, dated 1380, which includes '*un grant cuiller à dresser viande, les deux pommeaux verres*' (a big basting spoon, with two enamelled pommels). Once again, the spoon has two pommels, but there is no indication as to their position. It is one of the minor mysteries of the Middle Ages, among the host of more important ones.

To summarize it all, it can safely be stated that before the end of the fourteenth century, Europe had produced several types of

A set of 14th-century French spoons, with their stems terminated with acorn or diamond points. *Victoria and Albert Museum, London*

spoons whose production was to continue during the following centuries. Among them are spoons in silver, gold, pewter, bronze and latten. At first they have circular bowls, then in the late thirteenth century the bowls become elongated, but always with straight stems or square, round or hexagonal section, sometimes very short, as in the case of the popular 'fist spoon'. The end of the stem was cut at right-angles in the simplest type. Others were decorated with finials, which could be figures of an object or animal. Acorns, diamond points and sometimes precious stones also ornamented the tops of the stems. Some mediaeval spoons were decorated in enamel, some had engraved coats of arms. The short-stemmed fist spoons mostly carried the same type of decoration as the long-stemmed ones, and they often had the bowl attached to the stem with a lion's or dragon's head. Some mediaeval spoons were made in rare materials such as rock crystal, serpentine, cornelian and probably other types of semi-precious stones. Feeding and folding spoons also existed before the end of the fourteenth century. Finally, a strange type spoon decorated with the hoof of an animal was also made at a very early date, probably as early as the thirteenth century. Spoons of the Middle Ages are very rare indeed on the market, and the average collector has no hope of acquiring one, unless of course he is very lucky, for every serious collector knows that nothing is impossible and miracles sometimes happen. But most of those very early spoon types continued to be made for many centuries, and nobody could dismiss as a mere reproduction a folding spoon, acorn spoon or diamond-point spoon made during the sixteenth or even the seventeenth century.

Glossary of Early Mediaeval Spoons

Acorn spoon. One of the most popular spoons of the early Middle Ages, not only in Britain but all over the Continent. Appeared at the very beginning of the fourteenth century, but probably has an older origin. The type was made until the seventeenth century. The acorn spoon got its name from the decoration at the top of its stem. Different varieties are known. The acorn sometimes sprouts from a bunch of foliage or from a twisted orle.

Armorial spoon. Gold or silver spoons decorated with engravings of the owner's coat of arms, inside the bowl or on its reverse, are mentioned in documents as early as the beginning of the fourteenth century. Armorial spoons with stems decorated with enamelled coats of arms are also mentioned.

Ball or pommel spoon. A type often mentioned in documents of the fourteenth century, but with no full description, except that the stem was decorated with two balls (or pommels), sometimes enamelled.

Cut-end spoons. Very early type of spoon with normal square or hexagonal section stem with the end cut at right-angles. Very often in bronze, as they were a cheap type of spoon. Existed in the twelfth century.

Diamond-point finial spoon. A type of spoon which has appeared very early on the Continent, probably in the twelfth century. It reached England later, during the fourteenth century. It has a pointed knop, faceted like a diamond, at the end of its stem.

Drageoir spoon. A type of spoon which existed in France during the thirteenth century and is mentioned in many contemporary documents, wills and inventories. Its description is not given in any of the related documents. The spoon was used to eat *dragees*, a sweet which still exists as an almond covered with coloured sugar. Of course it might have been a different type of sweet in the Middle Ages.

Feeding spoon. A type of spoon called *cuiller a biberon* in French and which is mentioned in French documents as early as the fourteenth century. Some authors doubt whether these spoons were really used to feed infants or sick persons, and consider that they may have been used instead of a sauce boat. Later examples have the form of a circular scoop with a short curved handle. This type was still made in the sixteenth century. Proper feeding spoons appeared in England at the end of the seventeenth century.

Fist spoon. Otherwise known as *'vuistlepel'* in Dutch, *'cuiller de poing'* in French. A very early type of spoon, made on the Continent between the twelfth and sixteenth century, not only in silver but in pewter, latten and brass also. It has a very short stem and kept its circular bowl even as late as the sixteenth century. Very often decorated with a figure at the top of its stem, starting in the fifteenth century.

Folding spoon. This well-known type of spoon, equipped with a hinged stem enabling it to be folded in two, was very popular during the early Middle Ages. It appeared at the very beginning of the fourteenth century, and is often mentioned in contemporary documents. Mostly made in silver, it continued to be made until the eighteenth century. Rare in English silver, but quite common on the Continent.

Hoof spoon. Mysterious type of spoon which existed in western Europe as early as the thirteenth century, but it is probably much older. Everything points to an eastern Mediterranean origin. Was still being made, notably in Holland, during the eighteenth century. Most extant examples are in silver, but older examples are in bronze. The stem of the spoon is usually slightly curved, and its top is decorated with the hoof of an animal (horse, goat, etc.).

Luxury spoons. Spoons made out of rock crystal, semi-precious stones such as serpentine or cornelian, or gold and silver with a finial of precious stones, existed in the fourteenth century and are often mentioned in wills or inventories. Such luxury spoons continued to be made well into the sixteenth century and even later.

Picture spoon. Called *'cuiller à ymaiges'* in Old French, which could be rendered as 'picture spoon' in English, although the term has never been adopted in England. These early spoons have the tops of their stem decorated with figures, animals, saints, buildings, etc. They do appear in the fourteenth century, but it was mainly during the fifteenth that they became popular, and they have remained so for a very long time—in fact they never stopped being made. They can be found in silver, pewter or brass. The most famous is the apostle spoon, which appeared during the fifteenth century.

Spice spoon. A type of spoon very often mentioned in French documents of the thirteenth century, but only by name, and unfortunately without any description.

4 SPOONS OF THE FIFTEENTH AND SIXTEENTH CENTURIES

On the evidence of the inventories and wills of the time, the fifteenth century was certainly a glorious period for the production of fine spoons. The Low Countries particularly produced some magnificent examples during the period of the duchy of Burgundy, the richest court in Europe at the time, in the fifteenth century. It was also the great period of *dinanderie*, a generic term which includes all kinds of objects in brass and copper, and craftsmen centred on the town of Dinant and in the Meuse valley produced spoons and many other kitchen utensils. The brass founders of the Meuse valley acquired quite a reputation for their brassware which was exported all over Europe. Of course, as most of these objects were not marked, it would be difficult today to attribute brass spoons, whatever they look like, to the craftsmen of Dinant. But others—silversmiths, goldsmiths, jewellers—competed during the century to produce the most lavish spoons imaginable, not only in Burgundy but in France, Italy and Germany.

In the inventory of the Duke of Berry, a great patron of the arts, written in the year 1416, are descriptions of some extraordinary spoons, enough to make a collector's mouth water. Among the many entries recorded by Victor Gay are the following:

> two spoons in gold, one with a spiral stem, one engraved with the letter J on the reverse of the bowl, weighing together 3 ounces;
> one spoon in serpentine, with a stem in crystal, together with a small fork, in a leather sheath;
> one spoon in crystal, with a folding stem, in a leather sheath;
> one spoon in horn, in a silver-studded sheath;
> one spoon in cornelian, with a silver stem;
> one spoon in gold, with a short stem, decorated in enamels with the coat of arms of the earl of Etampes.

In the inventory of the royal castle of Vincennes, near Paris, written in 1418 and mentioned by Henri Harvard, it is pleasant to rediscover the spoon with a twisted spiral stem and two enamelled balls (or pommels) which belonged to Queen Jehanne de Bourbon, already mentioned in the inventory of 1385. But other spoons are mentioned, including what must have been a masterpiece, a spoon in silver with a thick short stem and a finial in the shape of an enamelled swan. There is also mention of a spoon in gold, with six small pearls and one big one along the stem and a ruby at the end of it.

These luxury spoons, many of which were already being produced during the fourteenth century, are mentioned in countless wills and inventories all through the fifteenth and sixteenth centuries. Unfortunately they have almost all disappeared, the pearls and precious stones reutilized by jewellers to make other jewels, the gold and the silver melted down.

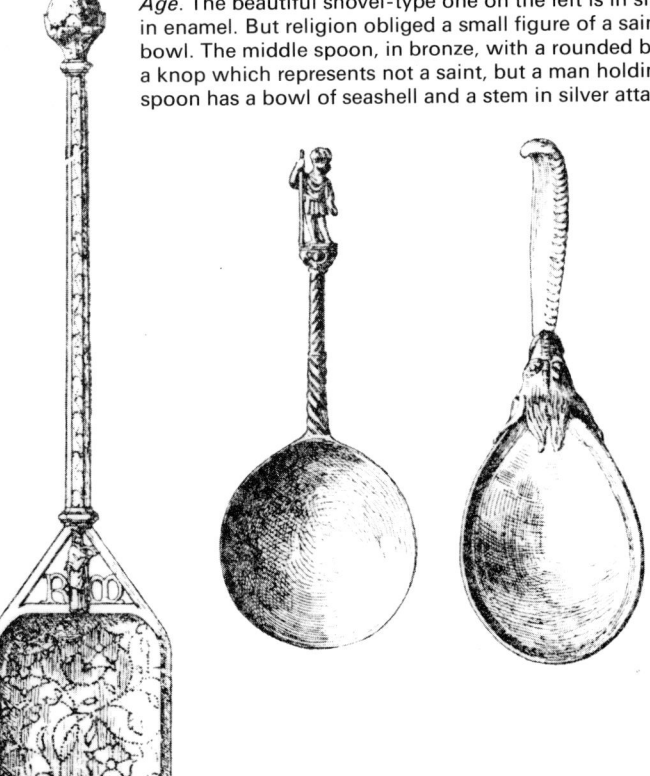

Three 15th-century spoons published by Victor Gay in his *Glossaire Archeologique du Moyen Age*. The beautiful shovel-type one on the left is in silver gilt, the stem terminated by a berry in enamel. But religion obliged a small figure of a saint at the junction of the stem with the bowl. The middle spoon, in bronze, with a rounded bowl and tapering twisted spiral stem, has a knop which represents not a saint, but a man holding a long staff in his right hand. The third spoon has a bowl of seashell and a stem in silver attached to the bowl by a rams head.

35

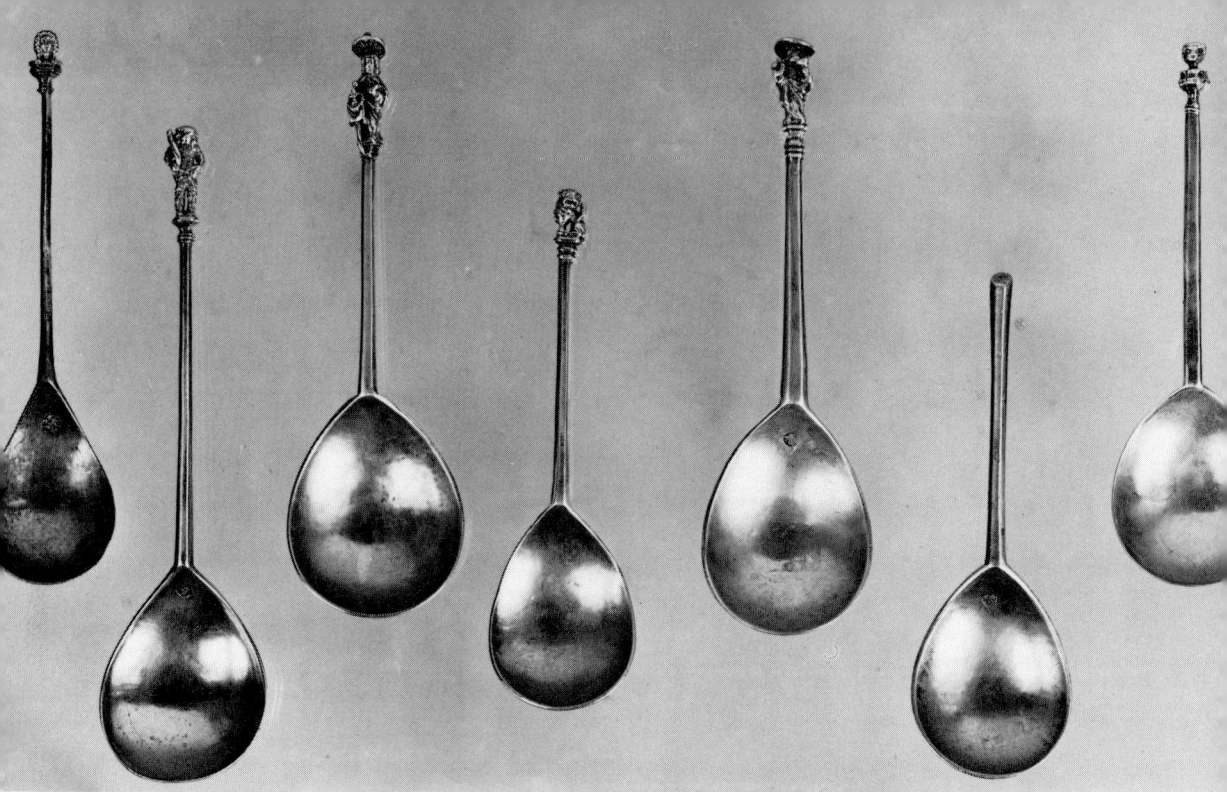

A fine selection of English knop spoons in silver. From left to right: maidenhead spoon from the end of the 14th century; wodewose knop spoon bearing the London hallmark of 1468; apostle spoon with the figures of St James the Great, from the second half of the 15th century; Lion sejeant spoon, from the 15th century, mark of a closed helmet; apostles spoon with the figure of St John, London hallmark for 1514–1515; slipped end spoon, with the London hallmark for 1525 and a maidenhead spoon, the head issuing from foliage, circa 1520. *Courtesy Victoria and Albert Museum, London*

The inventory of the Duke of Berry reveals that in many cases spoons were kept in sheaths, often made of leather, as early as the late fourteenth century. References to these leather sheaths are found all through the fifteenth century. The French royal accounts, dated 1489, contain the following note: 'To Jehan Barateau, sheath maker at Tours, a leather sheath decorated with the arms of France, to keep the silver spoons used at the king's table'. A reference in the inventory of the bishop of Senlis, dated 1496, reads: 'A leather sheaf in which 12 silver spoons have been found, each one with a strawberry as a finial, weighing together $11\frac{1}{2}$ ounces'. These examples, chosen among many entries in fifteenth-century documents, show that in very many cases the spoons were kept in sheaths often decorated with the owner's coat of arms, and silver-studded. The inventory of the bishop of Senlis is even more remarkable than some others, for it reveals the existence at the end of the fifteenth century of spoons with a strawberry finial.

The fifteenth century also saw the advent of yet another type of spoon, although some authors believe that it was already being made in the fourteenth century, when spoons had been made with bowls in semi-precious stones or rock crystal. This was the spoon whose bowl consists of a seashell, the stem being silver or brass. In the inventory of one well-to-do French lady, dated 1474, there is 'a mother-of-pearl spoon enamelled in blue, with a silver stem'. The seashell bowl spoon soon became very popular and went on being made until well into the nineteenth century, the later examples being sold as souvenirs from the seaside. According to various French authors, including Victor Gay, in the fifteenth century this

Five spoons which are collectors' dreams. From left to right: a famous Flemish-Burgundian spoon, probably made for the court of Philip the Good, in the 15th century; a German silver gilt spoon with a cowrie shell bowl; a German spoon of jasper with mounts in enamelled gold; a spoon of unknown origin, with stem in silver and the bowl in rock crystal. *Courtesy Victoria and Albert Museum, London*

type of spoon became a specialty of the silversmiths of La Rochelle, on the Atlantic coast of France, although unfortunately the La Rochelle Museum and the town's antique dealers are unable to confirm the statement.

It is of course most likely that even during the fifteenth century these spoons were produced in places not far from the sea or from harbours where the seashells could be obtained without undue difficulty. Seashell spoons are found everywhere today, but as they are never marked it is impossible to date them. They exist in different varieties, all of them fragile. The first type has a seashell bowl and a rounded baluster stem with a small ball as a finial. In the other type the stem is attached to the bowl by a lion's head, a very early attachment. Some very nice specimens are mentioned in the 1596 inventory of the possessions of the duchess of Cleves. The entry mentions: '*8 cuillers de pourcellaines garnyes d'argent doré, 3 cuillers de pourcellaines garnies d'argent doré à meufles de lion, manegées de corail à branches, aux yeulx des quels meufles y a des urmelles*'. The text is written in Old French and is not very clear, the meaning of the words *manegees* and *urmelles* having to be guessed, but the translation could be as follows: '8 seashell spoons decorated with

Silver Lion Sejeant spoon, circa 1500, with a mark representing a fleur de lys. Probably Paris.
Copyright A.C.L., Brussels

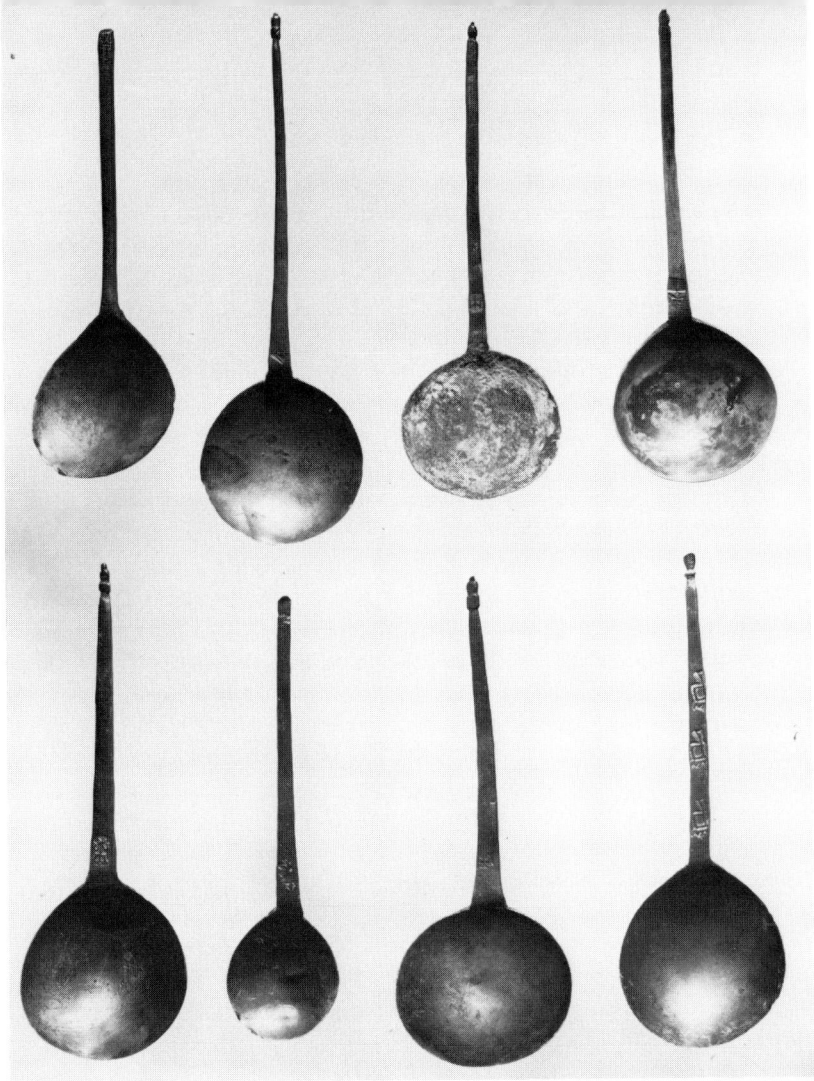

Series of eight brass spoons from the 15th and 16th centuries, Southern Low Countries. *Copyright A.C.L. Brussels*

silver, 3 seashell spoons decorated with silver gilt with lion's heads, with stems in coral, the lions' eyes being represented by *urmelles.*' Probably the *urmelles* were some kind of semi-precious stone. In his monumental *Glossaire d'Archeologie du Moyen-Age et de la Renaissance*, Victor Gay published a drawing of such a spoon, the seashell bowl attached to the silver feathershaped stem by a ram's head in silver.

Wonderful spoons continued to be made during the fifteenth and

39

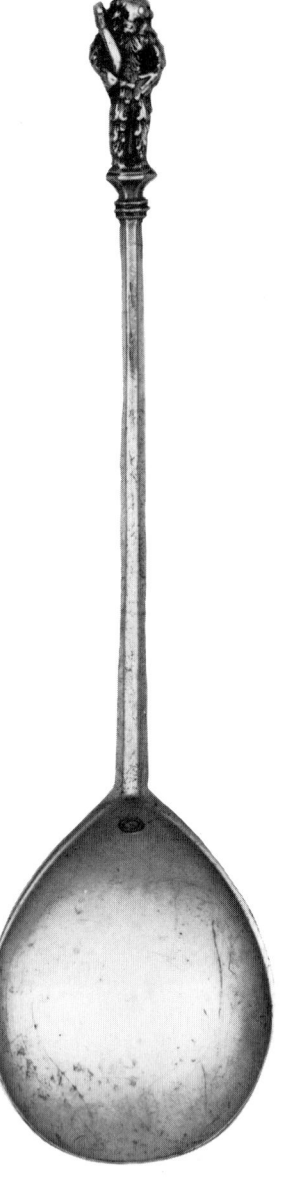

An extremely rare silver
'wodewose' spoon,
from the 15th century.
*Victoria and Albert
Museum, London*

especially the sixteenth century. The Louvre Museum has some of those rare beauties, including one which has a bowl carved out of maple wood, almond-shaped, and attached to a stem in silver gilt terminating in the figure of a woman with her arms crossed, the whole charming and elegant. The Cluny Museum has another sixteenth-century example with a bowl in agate attached to a silver gilt stem, with a miniature satyr in ruby as finial.

Thousands of such spoons were made, but they have nearly all been lost. If one was to appear in a sale room, it would fetch a terribly high price, beyond the reach of the average collector. Where have they all gone, all those beautiful spoons we read about in old documents? Where today are the coral spoons that Catherine de Medici kept in a malachite box at the end of the sixteenth century? Where are all the spoons that belonged to the great French writer Michel de Montaigne, who had four spoons with coral stems and bowls of mother-of-pearl? The list of owners of such great spoons would be endless. Spoons decorated with precious stones, pearls, enamels, silver and gold, spoons which were more jewels than table utensils, were made in France, Italy, the Low Countries and above all in Germany. It seems that this vogue did not take hold in England as much as it did on the Continent, but of course there were some made in England, and we know that King Edward VI, in 1549, was the owner of some marvellous spoons, including 'spones of cristall garnysshed wt gold enameled'.

One type of spoon belonging to the fifteenth century, probably made for the court of the Duke of Burgundy, is worth mentioning although extant examples are very rare. Those spoons, in silver gilt, were decorated with painted animals in white against dark-blue or black backgrounds. One of them, now in the Boston Museum of Fine Arts, is 17·5 cm long and had a fig-shaped bowl decorated with a scene of a fox preaching to geese, while another fox seizes one of them. The spoon is described in the catalogue of the exhibition of 'Flanders in the Fifteenth Century' held in Detroit in 1960. All the tiny figures reproduced are in white against a blue background, with raining stars in white and gold. The bowl is attached to the stem by a silver gilt head. The stem is of the twisted spiral type. There is another, smaller, spoon of this type in the Victoria and Albert Museum in London, on which a monkey is represented riding a stag in what

40

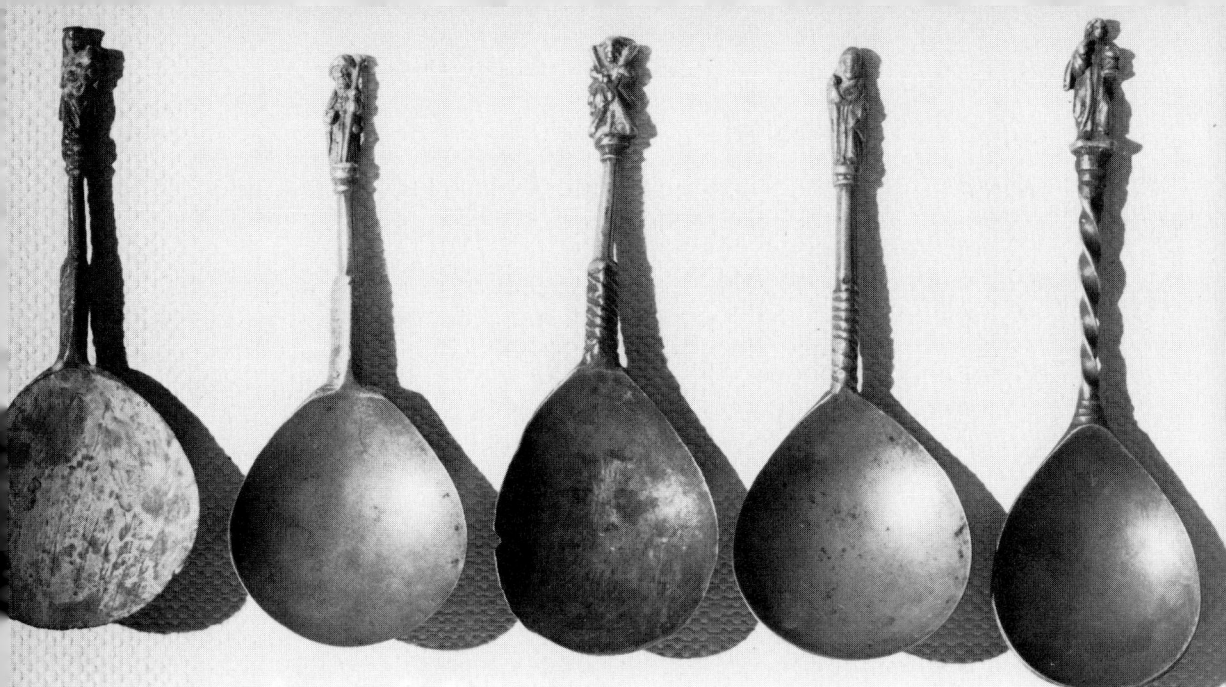

looks like a forest. These spoons, probably of Flemish origin, and called Burgundian, were probably made in the fifteenth century for Burgundian nobles, if not for the court of Philip the Good.

The collector who discovered a spoon of this Flemish type would be very lucky indeed. But one must not forget that spoons made during the fifteenth and sixteenth centuries were not all of the luxury type, as only a select few could afford such luxuries in an era when the vast majority of people was poor and often faced near-starvation. More democratic spoons were made of wood first, but also in cheaper metals such as brass, pewter and bronze. They have no decoration at all, just a bowl and a straight stem *'a bout coupé'* (with a cut end). All these simple spoons, even some made in silver, were never marked and it is therefore very difficult to give them a birth certificate. They can be found in many museums, and the Brussels Museum, for instance, has some very good examples in bronze.

We have decided to use the term 'picture spoon' to translate the French *'cuiller a ymaiges'*, used during the Middle Ages to designate spoons which were decorated with a miniature figure on top of the stem. The most famous of these was the apostle spoon, which appeared in an era when even people of low extraction were

Five apostle spoons in brass with finials representing respectively the Virgin, St James the More, St Andrew, St James the Less, and St John. *Musée Diocesain Liège;* Copyright *A.C.L., Brussels*

41

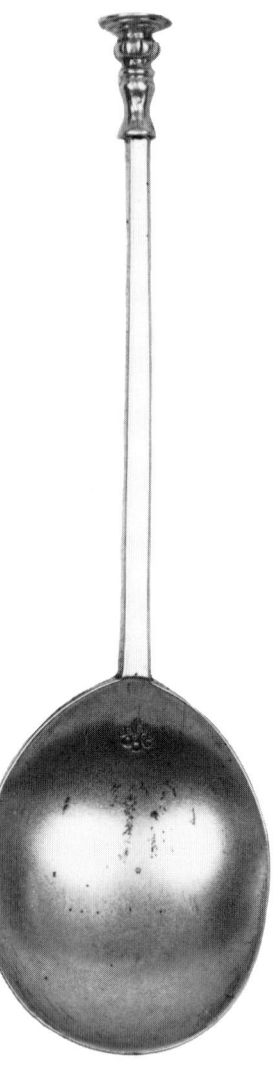

English slip-top spoon. *Victoria and Albert Museum, London*

profoundly religious. In the Middle Ages, architecture was the dominating art. Those masterpieces of mediaeval goldsmiths, the reliquaries, were miniature churches, and cathedrals were giant reliquaries. The style of mediaeval furniture was inspired by religious architecture, and cathedral facades were represented on it, with unnecessary gables, pointed arches and rose-windows. The backs of chairs represented church fronts. On the mediaeval churches and cathedrals were carved stone statues of saints, strange animals, odd creatures. The isolated figures are uniform, stiff and lifeless, with simple gestures and faces without expression. But saints were not carved only in stone, they were also carved in wood. In fact saints were everywhere.

Apostle spoons—the correct term should be saint spoons—spoons decorated with a miniature figure of a saint on top of the stem, belong to a time when in every household prayers were said before and after meals. All saints were venerated, and they were often considered to have power to influence people's lives. There is nothing astonishing in the fact that contemporary spoons were decorated with figures of saints, male and female, as well as those of Christ, the Virgin Mary, the Virgin and Child and a few others. Those spoons fit exactly in to the mediaeval framework.

In all probability, it is somewhere around the middle of the fifteenth century that saint spoons started to be produced, although picture spoons had been made during the fourteenth century, not only in silver but also, in greater numbers, in pewter and in latten. The saint spoon appeared simultaneously all over Christian Europe. Mentioned for the first time in an English text in 1494, it is of universal character and is found in Britain, France, Germany and Italy as well as in the Low Countries. The bowls of the earlier models in particular are often circular, both in the fifteenth and also the sixteenth century, but most of them have fig-shaped bowls, whether they are in silver or in pewter. The miniature statues of saints which decorate the tops of the stems are identical, when closely examined, to the stone and wooden statues of the period.

Many British authors state that these spoons were given as birth presents to newborn babies and that they were sometimes offered as a set of thirteen, made up of the twelve apostles and Christ, known as the Master. Unfortunately the latter statement is not substantiated

by contemporary texts, either in England or on the Continent. It is probable that apostle spoons were given as birth presents, and the Dutch still give them today, although these are of teaspoon size. The first saint spoons, like all other picture spoons, had a length of approximately 13 cm (even smaller when they were of the fist spoon type), but the length increased steadily to reach some 20 cm in the seventeenth century. That they were given, and therefore sold, as sets of thirteen is still to be proved. A very few such sets exist, and these are all of British origin, and always in silver, whereas many more saint spoons were made in cheaper metals. It is logical to think that silversmiths and other metal workers made saint spoons to be

Four French 15th-century spoons, including two with diamond-point finial and two with acorn top finial. *Victoria and Albert Museum, London*

Fabulous Burgundian (Flemish) spoon from the 15th century, a remarkable example of historical decoration in enamel on silver. The scene painted inside the bowl represents a monkey riding a stag in a forest. *Courtesy Victoria and Albert Museum, London*

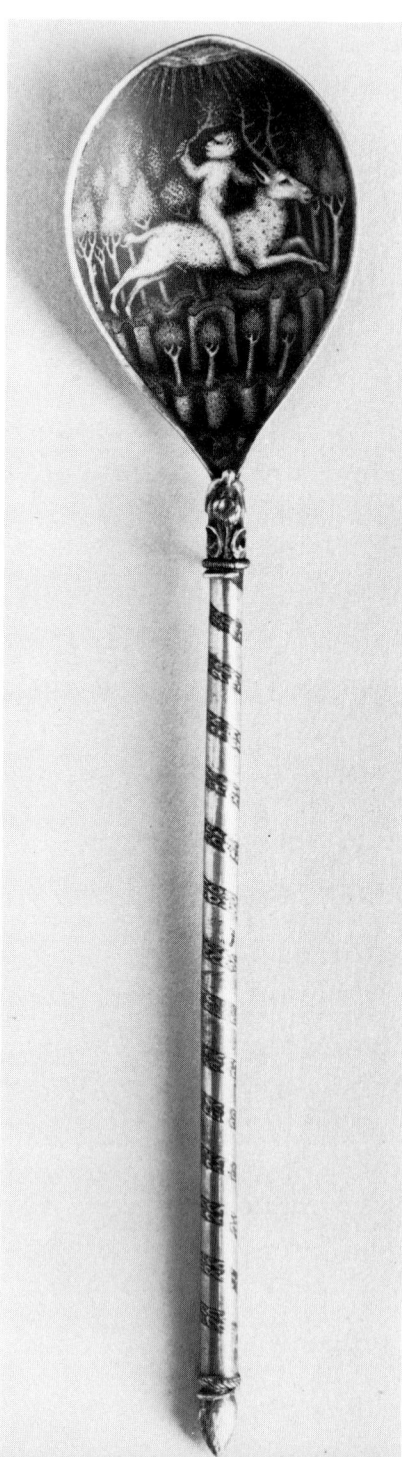

A very unusual spoon in brass, the top of the stem terminated by a figure of St Andrew holding his cross. Flemish, 15th century. *Byloke Museum, Ghent; copyright A.C.L., Brussels*

bought one by one. Customers could therefore buy as many as they liked and assemble them if they wished.

Most of the known sets of thirteen have spoons which are not in fact decorated with figures of the apostles. The real apostles, twelve in number, were Peter, Andrew, James the Greater, James the Less, John, Philip, Bartholomew, Matthew, Thomas, Simon, Jude and Judas. Judas, for obvious reasons, was always omitted and is replaced by St Matthias, who can be considered as one of the original apostles. But in certain sets St Paul takes the place of St Jude, or St Mark or St Luke replaces St Matthias, which logically indicates that sets with twelve apostles were not produced, since in the Middle Ages everybody knew very well who the apostles were. The British sets of thirteen are very rare. They include one from 1617, now in the possession of the Worshipful Company of Goldsmiths, in London, and another of the same late date in the Henry Ford Museum, Dearborn, USA. A third set is in the collection of the Francis E Fowler Museum, Beverley Hills, California. The oldest, dated 1450, is in Christ's Hospital, London.

As has been mentioned, other saints than the apostles were reproduced on spoons—saints such as St Paul, St Mark, St Luke and a few others just as respectable, such as St Joseph and St John the Baptist. A few woman saints appeared too, such as St Barbara and St Catherine. It is very likely that the mediaeval guilds possessed spoons decorated with figures representing their patron saint. The London Merchant Taylors Company, whose patron was St John the Baptist, is recorded in an inventory carried out in 1512 as owning a set of spoons in silver decorated with the figure of St John. The London Innholders Company still has a collection of twenty-one spoons, also in silver, decorated with the figure of St Julian. The Dutch guilds also had their 'gilde lepels', and many are still extant, but most of them are decorated with miniature statues, not of saints, but of a working man using the tools used in everyday life by the guild members. In certain cases the spoon knop is composed of a single tool, such as a pair of scissors.

The saintly figures appearing as knops on spoons can only be identified by the emblems carried and generally associated with individual saints. Christ, the Master, carries the orb and cross, St John a cup and St Andrew a saltire cross. St Peter of course is always represented with his keys of the Kingdom, St Bartholomew with flaying knife, St Matthias with an axe, St Thomas with a spear. St James the Greater always has a pilgrim's staff, St James the Less a fuller's bat, St Philip a short cross, St Jude a processional cross, St Simon Zelotes a saw, St Matthew a carpenter's square or even a purse. It sometimes takes a lot of research to identify certain male or female saints through the emblems they carry, and in some cases it has been impossible to do it, even after going through many dictionaries of Christian iconography.

Most of the saint spoons produced on the Continent carry more elaborate decoration than the British examples, very often with a complementary figure at the bottom of the stem, just above the attachment which connects stem to bowl. The bowls are very often engraved with foliage, fruit, sometimes even coats of arms. In some cases the name of the saint is engraved on the side of the stem. Another very important difference is that on British spoons the saints always, or nearly always, have a halo, which is hardly ever found, except in a very few rare cases, on the Continent. In the early examples of British saint spoons, the halo consists of a silver disc, often pierced, placed at the back of the head; in later examples the disc is put horizontally on the saint's head. Again, the Continent, mainly France and the Low Countries, often produced short-stemmed saint spoons of the 'first' type, which do not seem to be recorded in Britain.

If the continental saints represented on spoons do not carry a halo, many more saints were represented. And many of those saints are found on convent spoons, for everything points to the fact that when they entered the convent nuns presented a spoon with the effigy of their patron saint on top of the stem. The Brussels Museum of Art and History has some of these wonderful spoons in its collections, all of them with fig-shaped bowls. One has the bowl attached to the stem by means of a short rat-tail, and the inside of the bowl decorated with a thread and a gilt border. The stem, of square section, terminates in the figure of a female saint with a basket under her right arm and carrying a jar in her left hand. She has the rare continental attribute of a halo, and has not been identified yet. The reverse of the bowl is engraved with a banderole with the inscription 'Sr Jenme Duquesne' above the date, 1607. The spoon is well hallmarked and was made by Antoine Desurmont, a silversmith of Tournai. A second spoon, identical to the first but not hallmarked, has a banderole of a different type engraved on the reverse of the bowl with the inscription 'Sr Jeanne Dalost' and the date 1607.

A third silver spoon in the same Brussels collection, with the Antwerp hallmark, has a stem of square section with the inscription 'Sr Catherine Rusette 1607'. The stem terminates with the gilt figure of St Catherine of Alexandria with the Emperor Maxentius at her feet. She has a book in her right hand and a halo at the back of her head. The bowl is decorated with engravings of fruit and foliage. A fourth spoon in the collection, from the late sixteenth century, has a square-section stem terminated by a sphere with two threads in the middle. The reverse of the bowl is inscribed 'Sr Jeanne Gervais'. A fifth spoon, in silver, has a square-section stem terminated by a strawberry sprouting from four leaves. The spoon is inscribed 'Sr Anne Dubois 1628'. The last spoon in this interesting set has a square-section stem attached to the bowl by a very thin rat-tail. The back of the bowl is inscribed 'Sr Marie Le Poivre' above the date, 1604. Whoever Marie Le Poivre was, the stem of her spoon is terminated by a gilt Virgin and Child, quite normal in this case because the owner's patron saint is the Virgin Mary.

In all five cases, the owner's name is preceded by the initials 'Sr', for 'soeur' (sister). It is most likely that those spoons were given to convents by young girls who had taken the veil.

All but one of the Brussels Museum convent spoons are probably from the end of the sixteenth century, the inscriptions being of a later date. Spoons decorated with figures of female saints are not rare by any means, at least on the Continent: without looking too far, the author knows of one in a private collection in Brussels, decorated with a beautiful gilt figure of St Barbara and made by an Antwerp silversmith in the early seventeenth century. The Musée Diocesain in Liège has a brass spoon from the mid-seventeenth, its stem terminating with the figure of a female saint who has not been identified. The same museum also has three other fifteenth-century spoons of the knop type, decorated with the figures of St James the Greater, St James the Less and St Andrew. The lucky owner of the St Barbara spoon has another decorated with the figure of St Romoldus, a very rare saint on spoons. The Brussels Museum has a marvellous silver spoon from the end of the sixteenth century, with a fig-shaped bowl and square-section stem terminated by the figure of St Anthony, who holds a staff in one hand and a book in the other and has a pig at his feet. A coat of arms is engraved inside the bowl and on the reverse is the inscription: 'To the hospital of Our Lady of Lessines' (Lessines is a small town south of Brussels). The same inscription appears on a spoon decorated with the Virgin and Child, which reveals the existence of still another possibility. Those spoons are all addressed to a hospital which was run by nuns, and it is possible that such spoons were given to the hospital by cured patients.

But there is a spoon type which is probably older than the saint type and which appears to be exclusively British. It is a spoon decorated with a woman's head on top of the stem, known as a maidenhead

Silver spoon from the end of the 16th century with a new circular bowl and square section stem. The finial is composed of a sphere encircled by two threads in slight relief. The reverse of the bowl is engraved with the name 'S.R. Jeanne Gervais'. Southern Netherlands. *Copyright A.C.L., Brussels*

spoon. Like the apostle spoons, the maidenhead spoon was produced in Britain until the seventeenth century. It is first recorded at the beginning of the fifteenth century, but could well date from the end of the fourteenth. Its origin is somewhat obscure, but like the hoof spoon it seems to have originated somewhere in the region of the eastern Mediterranean, for the Victoria and Albert Museum houses a very rare spoon with an elongated fig-shaped bowl and a diamond-section stem terminated with a female head. This spoon, found in excavations carried out in Coventry, is punched with the arms of the kings of Jerusalem. Similar spoons have also been found in Greece, and they all seem to date from the thirteenth century, so it may be that travellers to the East brought back hoof spoons and these so-called maidenhead spoons, which were then copied in western Europe, mainly in Britain. But if the maidenhead spoon is of very ancient origin, it would be hard to discover one example made before the sixteenth century.

Many inventories and wills contain references to these famous maidenhead spoons. Some authors have advanced the theory that the head is the Virgin Mary's, but there is no documentary evidence to corroborate the hypothesis. In many instances, the top of the maidenhead spoon is decorated with the bust of a woman rising out the calyx of a fleur de lys. Since the iconography of the Middle Ages contains no known example of the Virgin Mary being represented by the bust of a woman, it is doubtful that the maidenhead is such a representation. Furthermore, none of the recorded maidenheads are decorated with a halo of sanctity. The maidenhead spoon is a typical British product, although spoons decorated with heads or busts of women were made on the Continent. Henri d'Allemagne prints a picture of such a spoon, whose stem looks like a caryatid terminated by the head of a woman. This bronze spoon is German and belongs to the sixteenth century.

If the maidenhead spoon is unlikely to bear the representation of the Holy Virgin, other spoons decorated with the Virgin and with the Virgin and Child certainly were made during the fifteenth and sixteenth centuries, not only in silver but also in brass. The type is very rare in English silver but common on the Continent. Made mainly in the Low Countries, France, Italy and Germany, they went out of fashion well before the end of the seventeenth century.

Most British references mention the existence of only three spoons of the type: one of them, dated 1577, is in the Victoria and Albert Museum in London; the Holburne of Menstrie Museum in Bath has one of the Virgin and Child type, and a third, of the Virgin and Sacred Heart type, was sold by Sotheby's in 1954. But many, many continental museums have spoons of this type. For instance there are three in the small Musée Diocesain in Liège (Belgium) alone, all made of brass. The first is fifteenth-century and of the straight Holy Virgin type. It is 17 cm long, with a fig-shaped bowl. The other two, decorated with the Virgin and Child, belong to the sixteenth century and are much shorter than the first, measuring only 13 cm in length.

The Brussels Museum of Arts and History has a more lavish late sixteenth-century example of silver, with the Virgin and Child. It is 19 cm long and has a fig-shaped bowl, with a square-section stem attached by a short rat-tail. The Virgin, in gilt, holds the Child in her right arm. The back of the bowl was later decorated with the engraving of a coat of arms above the date 1605. Inside the bowl is the French inscription: 'To the hospital of Our Lady of Lessines'. The H. J. E. van Beuningen Museum, in Rotterdam, also has a silver spoon, from the first quarter of the seventeenth century, with the Virgin and Child.

Spoons with the Virgin and Virgin and Child are by no means rare in museums, but another type, the Holy Family, is among the rarest of all. We know that there was at least one, whose whereabouts are today unknown, in the collection of a certain Louis Minard, architect in the town of Ghent, in the second quarter of the nineteenth century. Minard, who had a marvellous collection of fifteenth- and sixteenth-century spoons, had a silver one, sixteenth-century and probably Flemish, decorated with the Virgin and Child and St Joseph. The stem was composed of two entwined branches, a very unusual type.

Nothing is more logical than to find lions decorating spoons in the Middle Ages and in the Renaissance, for the lion was a much-used decorative motif in architecture, and appeared on countless coats of arms of princedoms, dukedoms and earldoms, as well as cities and even provinces. It is even represented on furniture—on armchairs, tables, cupboards. And if the lion is ever present in the Middle Ages, the lion sejeant spoon is one of the most decorative and most eagerly sought after.

The lion sejeant spoon ('sejeant' means 'sitting' in the heraldic vocabulary) has its stem topped with the figure (often in silver gilt) of a small lion sitting with straight forelimbs. The lion can be facing to the right, or facing to the front with a shield in front of him. The Victoria and Albert Museum has one of the oldest of these spoons, dating from the fifteenth century. Although created after the acorn, the maidenhead and the diamond-point spoons, the lion sejeant spoon must have appeared right at the beginning of the fifteenth century, but its existence is not recorded before the sixteenth. The famous Jewel Book of Henry VIII contains references to some beautiful examples, such as two spoons in gold decorated with lions holding a shield with the arms of the king in enamel, another one in gold, the stem enamelled, with a white lion at the top, a gold spoon with the figure of a lion holding a ring in his claws, and also five spoons in parcel gilt, three of them decorated with 'womens heddes', the other two with lions.

It seems that lion sejeant spoons were very popular in Tudor times and many were made in London and in the provinces. Like many other spoons of the fifteenth century, they went on being made until the end of the seventeenth. Collectors should know that, like other spoons of the period, they were also made in pewter and in latten as well as in gold or in silver.

Lion sejeant spoons were also made extensively on the Continent. The Brussels Museum has a beautiful example made circa 1500, with a lion holding a shield. It is 17·5 cm long, with a bowl in silver and stem in brass, with a spiral twist nearer the bowl, the rest being of hexagonal section. The Byloke Museum, in Ghent, has another lion sejeant spoon, also in silver, made in Maastricht (Holland) in the first quarter of the seventeenth century.

Lion sejeants, like maidenhead spoons, are very rare and seldom appear in salesrooms. Henry VIII seems to have loved spoons, for besides maidenhead spoons and gold lion sejeant spoons, according to his Jewel Book he also had spoons decorated with precious stones. The Book also contains references to certain types of spoon which have completely disappeared, such as spoons with angels on top of the stem, and with doves.

A great many picture spoons were made during the fifteenth and sixteenth centuries, in silver, bronze and pewter, but the extant examples are very rare today, as they were melted, buried or more simply just thrown away. Among these spoons is the famous British 'wodewose spoon', a silver spoon with a straight stem decorated with the figure of a 'wodewose' or 'wild man of the wood'. The Victorian and Albert Museum has one such spoon, dated circa 1460, and only two others are reported in Britain. Nobody knows who the wild man is. Some authors associate the image with the pre-Christian folk figure of 'the Green Man', others with 'the wild man of the woods', a mediaeval legend, while others advance the theory that it could be the representation of St John the Baptist. Whatever it is, the spoon exists and is very rare.

A very few examples of still another type of finial, the Moor's Head, made during the sixteenth century, are also recorded, but nobody seems to know for sure who the head represents. Other spoons with an owl finial are recorded not only in England but on the Continent as well, and a set of six belongs to Corpus Christi College, Oxford, all dated 1506.

At the end of the 16th century Scotland produced a type of spoon which is typical of the country, the disc-end spoon. This has a shallow rounded bowl and a flat stem, with a flat disc as the finial which was very often decorated with two or four initials. The earliest of these dates from 1565, and they continued to be made until the middle of the 17th century. A few examples have a death's head engraved on the disc, and some 17th century ones have an acanthus leaf engraved there. It is possible that the spoons stamped with initials were wedding spoons.

British collectors have always been keen on spoons, but the picture is quite different in continental countries, where nobody, or practically nobody, has ever bothered to trace, record and write about spoons. Yet the Continent provides an immense variety of finials on spoons of the fifteenth and sixteenth centuries. A leisurely search through documents and in a few museums has revealed the existence of spoons terminated with figures of angels, women's heads, wolves, rams' heads, nude women, antique warriors and owls. In the Bodo Glaub collection in Cologne, which has been exhibited quite a few times outside the country, there is a fifteenth-century spoon with stem terminating in an embracing couple, definitely one of the oldest known love spoons. Henri d'Allemagne published another, in bronze, also with an embracing couple on top of the stem, which was then attributed to the thirteenth century, but probably dates from two centuries later. Another bronze spoon of the fifteenth century is topped by a pineapple. Others are decorated with olives, various unidentified women, and grotesque masks.

In the sixteenth century, spoons began to be produced which were decorated not only with saints, including St Joseph and many others, but with allegorical figures such as Fortune, Love, Justice, Charity and Hope. Others are decorated with horses, sailing ships, cows, even dogs. Biblical figures are also reported, such as King David and Judith and Holofernes. Anyone who needed convincing of the variety of figures needs only to consult the famous Tichborne set of spoons, made in London in 1592. It consists of twelve spoons with stems topped by tiny figures of the 'worthies': in this case Christ, St Peter, King David, Judas Maccabaeus, Joshua, Alexander the Great, Charlemagne, Hector, Julius Caesar, King Arthur, Guy of Warwick and Queen Elizabeth. Each spoon was engraved with the name of the figure. The set unfortunately has disappeared from view since it was sold in 1914.

A search in European museums would probably reveal many other figures so far unrecorded, not only on silver spoons, but also on spoons in pewter, bronze and brass. The Italians produced some very fancy spoons in silver, with scalloped bowls and curved handles representing fauns. Each country showed its characteristic creative power, and silversmiths, whatever their country, are individuals with individual taste. But fifteenth- and sixteenth-century spoons were not always decorated with finials. Some are much simpler. And among the simplest, manufactured by all the silversmiths, pewterers and braziers of various countries, are the ball-knop spoons. Stems terminated by a ball were made in England, and one set of six, dated 1561, is in the collection of Corpus Christi College, Oxford. Ball-knop spoons were also made in the Low Countries, notably by the silversmiths of Antwerp, in France and in the Scandinavian countries. A rare type, and typically British, is the 'wrythen spoon', not found on the Continent, whose finial is formed as a ball engraved with spirally twisted fluting. These spoons appeared for the first time around the mid-fifteenth century, and

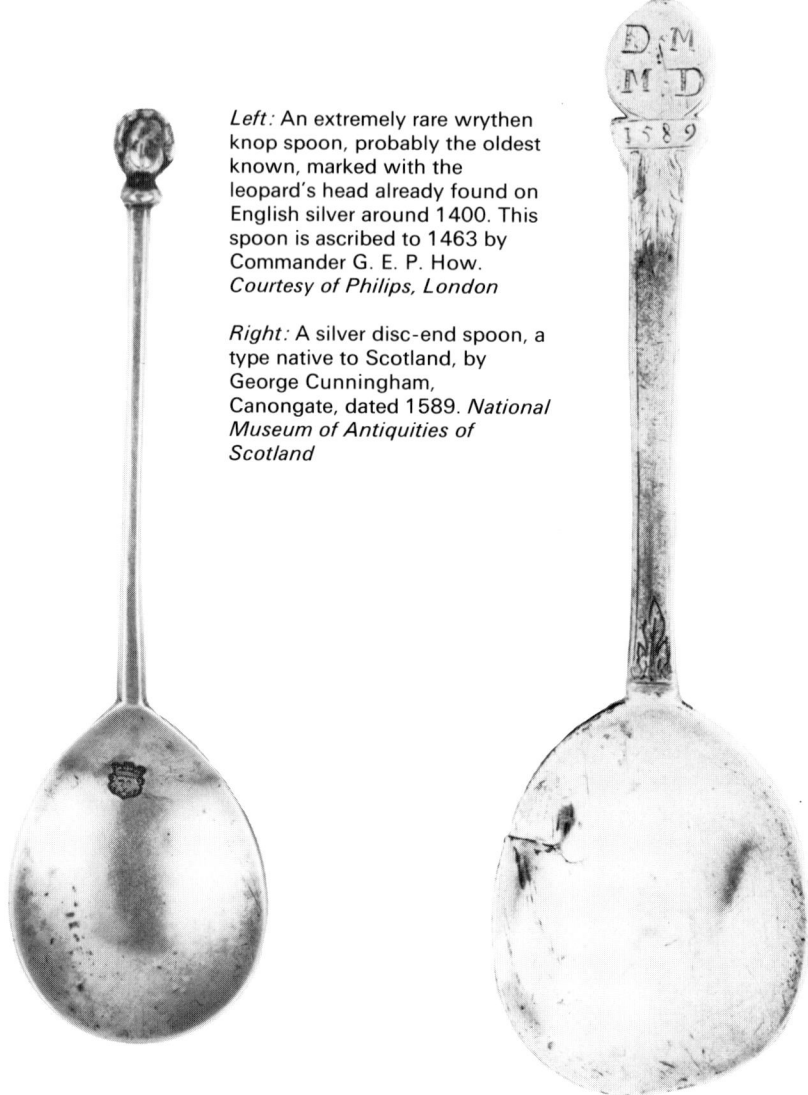

Left: An extremely rare wrythen knop spoon, probably the oldest known, marked with the leopard's head already found on English silver around 1400. This spoon is ascribed to 1463 by Commander G. E. P. How. *Courtesy of Philips, London*

Right: A silver disc-end spoon, a type native to Scotland, by George Cunningham, Canongate, dated 1589. *National Museum of Antiquities of Scotland*

apparently stopped being made a century later. They are terribly rare on the art market today.

The second half of the fifteenth century also saw the appearance of another type of very simple spoon, the 'slip-top spoon', made sometimes in silver, more often in pewter and brass. The end of the stem was cut at an acute angle, making enough space on top of the stem to engrave initials. The slip-top, like the wrythen-top spoon, stopped being made a century later and is also extremely rare, no doubt because it is not very elaborate and not attractive enough to be kept among family heirlooms. Yet another type of spoon, the 'seal-top', appeared at the end of the fifteenth century, in England and on the Continent. The spoon is decorated with a short finial in the shape of a hexagonal seal, which could also be engraved with initials. The type went right out of fashion around the middle of the seventeenth century, when other types made their appearance.

Glossary of Spoons of the Fifteenth and Sixteenth Centuries

Disc-end spoon. A type of spoon which was produced in Scotland and the northern counties of England, and which is most likely of Scandinavian origin. The spoon has a shallow bowl and a flat stem terminated by a disc. Some discs carry two initials, others a death's head. Earliest dates to circa 1565.

Lion sejeant spoon. Spoon with a top representing a seated lion, made in silver, pewter, latten and sometimes gold, and very popular in Tudor times. The seated lion may be facing the front or looking to the side. Later examples have the lion facing the front and holding a shield which is often engraved with various designs. Many examples in continental silver. Seems to have first appeared at the beginning of the sixteenth century; most of the English ones produced between 1520 and 1620. Some continental examples from the eighteenth century.

Luxury spoons. Spoons decorated with precious stones, with bowls made in rock crystal, serpentine, cornelian and other semi-precious stones. Most of them were made during the sixteenth century, and they are reported in countless inventories and wills, but they seem to have completely disappeared. They were usually made with stems in gold or silver, with cheaper examples in brass. Many fifteenth-century examples had the bowl attached to the stem by means of a lion, a dragon's head or a ram's head. Some are reported with coral stems.

Maidenhead spoon. A typically British spoon, of a type older even than the saint spoon. Appeared in the beginning of the fifteenth century and stopped being made around the mid-seventeenth century. The type may have originated somewhere in the region of the eastern Mediterranean. The finial is formed as the head and bust of a woman emerging from a calyx of foliage. Spoons decorated with a woman's head and bust were also made on the Continent during the same period.

Moor's head spoon. Rare spoon from the end of the fifteenth century, with hexagonal-section stem and fig-shaped bowl. So called because of the vague resemblance between the finial head and the heraldic Moor's Head. Might be the head of anybody: some authors believe that it actually represents the Holy Child, but really nobody knows. Spoons with male or female heads are very often found on the Continent during the sixteenth century.

Mother-of-pearl spoon. Spoon whose bowl consists of a seashell attached to a silver or a brass stem, and in some rare cases to a rock crystal stem. This type of spoon had probably first appeared during the fourteenth century, but many were made during the fifteenth and sixteenth centuries. Quantities of these spoons were made during the nineteenth century; none of them are marked.

Painted enamel spoon. A very rare type from the fifteenth century, typical of Flanders, with twisted spiral stem in silver. Both sides of the bowl were decorated with scenes painted in white against a black background.

Saint spoon. Spoon decorated with a figure of a saint, including the apostles, the Virgin, the Virgin and Child, the Virgin and Sacred Heart, at the top of the stem. These spoons are truly international: many countries made them, including France, Germany, the Low Countries and Italy. They started to appear around the mid-fifteenth century and remained fashionable until the end of the seventeenth, although quite a lot were made in the eighteenth century in Holland and Germany, and they are still made to this day. Of course saint spoons made after the seventeenth century are to be considered as reproductions of earlier types. They were made in silver, brass and pewter. Some of the fifteenth-century originals are of the fist-type, with very short stems and circular bowl. Most of them have fig-shaped bowls. Saints represented on spoons of British origin wear a halo, which is very rarely the case on the Continent. In many cases the saint is in silver gilt, the rest of the spoon in white silver.

Seal-top spoon. Appeared for the first time at the beginning of the sixteenth century in England and on the Continent, where quite a few examples are recorded. The stem finial terminates in a hexagonal seal, often engraved with initials. The type continued to be made in the following century, the seal becoming first oval then perfectly round.

Slip-top spoon. A type of spoon which appeared during the fifteenth century and ceased to be made around the middle of the following century. The stem finial is 'slipped' or cut at an acute angle, leaving space for the engraving of initials. Not reported on the Continent.

Sucket spoon and fork. See Chapter 7, on seventeenth-century spoons. The sucket spoon existed during the sixteenth century in Germany and the Low Countries, but became fashionable in the following century.

Virgin, Virgin and Child, Virgin and Sacred Heart, Holy Family spoon. Rare type in English silver, but not on the Continent. Associated of course with the Roman Catholic Church. Made from the mid-fifteenth century, until the first half of the seventeenth century. The figure (or figures) is very often in gilt, the rest of the spoon in white silver. The rarest is the Holy Family spoon, with a knop representing the Virgin and Child and St Joseph.

Wodewose spoon. A rare type of English spoon: only three are known. It has a figure finial of a man clad in skin and holding a club, probably a representation of the mythical forest spirit, the Green Man, although it may possibly depict St John the Baptist. None reported on the Continent, but the French author Victor Gay records one from the fifteenth century, in bronze, with a circular bowl attached to a twisted spiral stem.

Wrythen knop spoon. The finial of this spoon is formed as a ball engraved with spirally twisted fluting. Seems to have appeared in the fifteenth century and ceased to be made in the middle of the sixteenth century.

5 ANTIQUE SCANDINAVIAN SPOONS

Scandinavian spoons from the Middle Ages and the Renaissance are still seen occasionally in salesrooms or in antique shops, perhaps more often in Britain than anywhere else, although some beautiful examples in both silver and brass have lately appeared in Paris and in Brussels. The Scandinavians seem to have made silver spoons in great numbers, for they have always had a great love of silver, and not only the well-to-do people but even the poorer peasants, who likewise thought that silver was a good investment. Spoons could be found anywhere, in the households of the most remote villages and even in the barren land near the Arctic Circle, where the Norwegian and Swedish Lapps live.

The silver spoons of Scandinavia have certain characteristic differences from those produced in other parts of Europe, although they still followed some general European trends. But even in later periods, when they willingly adopted some general European styles, they still added their own details, decorative motifs taken from their own folklore and traditions. Like the French, the Germans and others, during the Middle Ages they produced fist spoons, with very short stems and fig-shaped bowls, and they went on making them

Above left: The inside of the bowl of a Danish silver gilt spoon, circa 1500.

Above right: The stem of the silver gilt spoon of circa 1500. The inside of the bowl is engraved with St Anne holding the infant Christ on her left knee with the Virgin to her right. The stem is mottled in imitation of a tree trunk, and is decorated with the instruments of the Passion. From the stem emerges the head of a man wearing a jewelled circlet. *Victoria and Albert Museum, London*

Below left: Reverse of the Danish silver gilt spoon. The reverse is engraved with a gothic A repeated three times; the stem is attached to the bowl by a tongue framed by a V shaped border. *Victoria and Albert Museum, London*

Below right: Back of the Danish silver gilt spoon of circa 1500. *Victoria and Albert Museum*

until the early seventeenth century, a bit later than the others. The fig-shaped bowl was retained even longer, until the beginning of the eighteenth century, when the oval-shaped bowl was finally adopted. The spoons made in the three Scandinavian countries have a certain similarity, which is not surprising in view of the fact that Norway and Denmark formed a single country until 1814, and that the Scanian provinces of Sweden belonged to Denmark until 1660.

In the fifteenth century, the silver or silver gilt spoons were mostly of the first type, no longer than 10 or 11 cm, with a very broad fig-shaped bowl engraved on both sides with religious scenes. The stems are attached to the bowl not by a rat-tail but by a long tongue in the form of a letter V, an attachment which is not found anywhere else. (Here the reader is referred to the collection of spoons held by the Victoria and Albert Museum, London.) Often the short

Danish silver spoon dated 1670. The reverse of the bowl is engraved with two sprays intertwined to form a wreath around the initial KMB, above the date 1670. The stem is terminated in a double rose. Length 17.2 cm. *Victoria and Albert Museum, London*

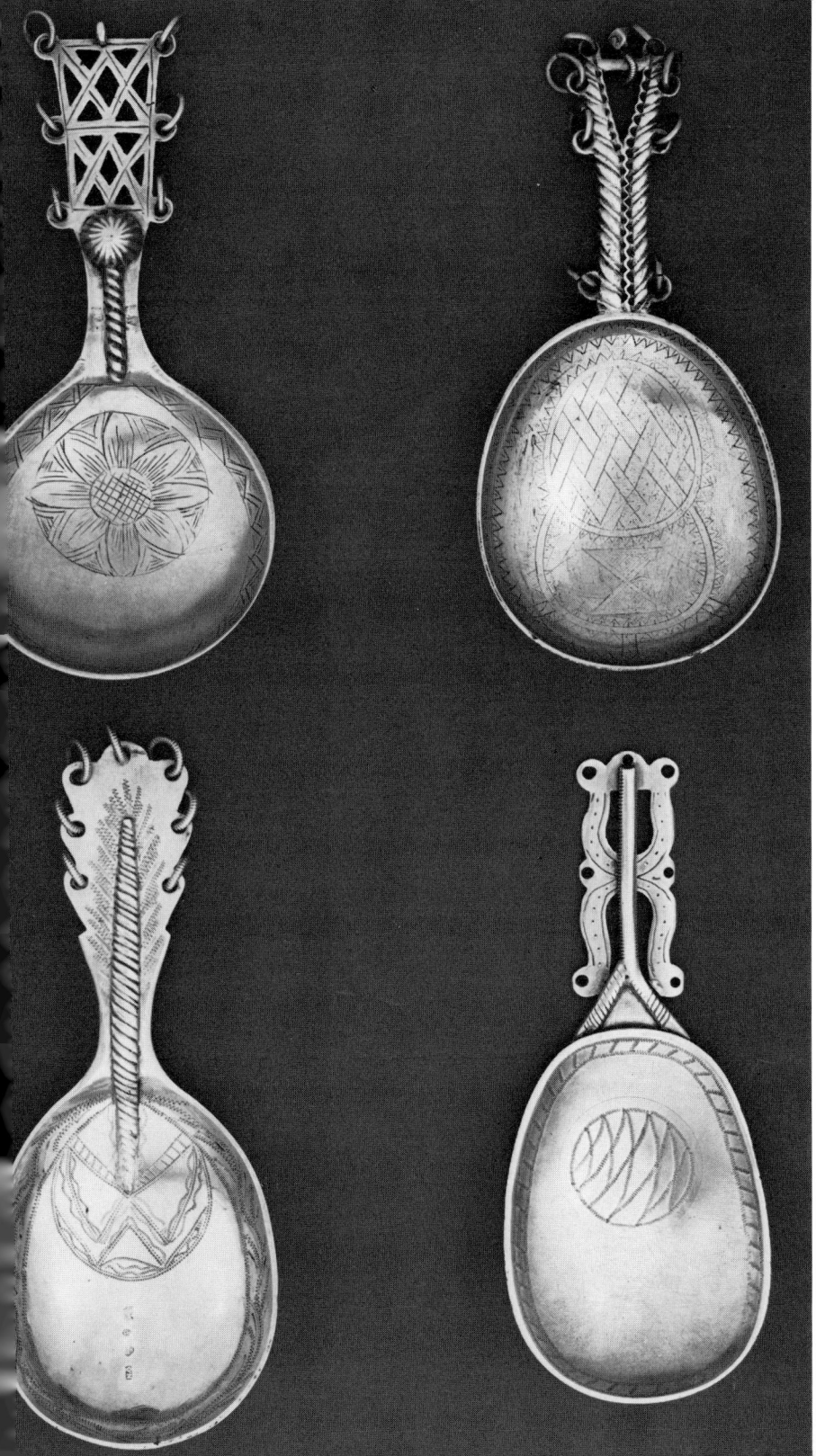

Norwegian and Swedish silver spoons made for the Lapp market. Above: Norwegian spoon, first half of the 18th century and Swedish silver spoon made in Lulea between 1805 and 1847 by Olof Forsberg. Bottom row: another Swedish silver spoon, second quarter of the 19th century, made by Nils Ohstedt of the town of Pitea, and another Norwegian mid-19th century silver spoon, made by Andreas Movelgang of Bergen. *Courtesy Victorian and Albert Museum, London*

Left: Two silver Danish spoons from the second half of the 18th century. The base of the stem, as so often happens in Scandinavia, is decorated with a moulded band. The top of the flat trefoil stem is scratch engraved with foliage. Dated 1769, length 19.6 cm. *Victoria and Albert Museum, London*

Below: Three 17th century Norwegian spoons. The middle one in pierced gilt of the 'fist type', with a rounded fig-shaped bowl, has a short stem with a flattened twisted pattern. The knop is composed from gothic strawberry leaves, with c rings. Length 15 cm. The left spoon, also from the second half of the 17th century has a rounded pear-shaped bowl. The knop is shaped as two cherub heads topped by a finial. The right hand trefid spoon is dated 1689. Both sides of the stem are engraved with a flowering spray, a tulip on the upper side, a rose on the lower. *Victoria and Albert Museum, London*

stems look very thick, as they were heavily decorated with all kinds of cast ornaments. As a matter of fact a thick stem would have given the user a firmer grip on the spoon, better than the case of the thin stems fashionable in other countries, but the ornamentation of the

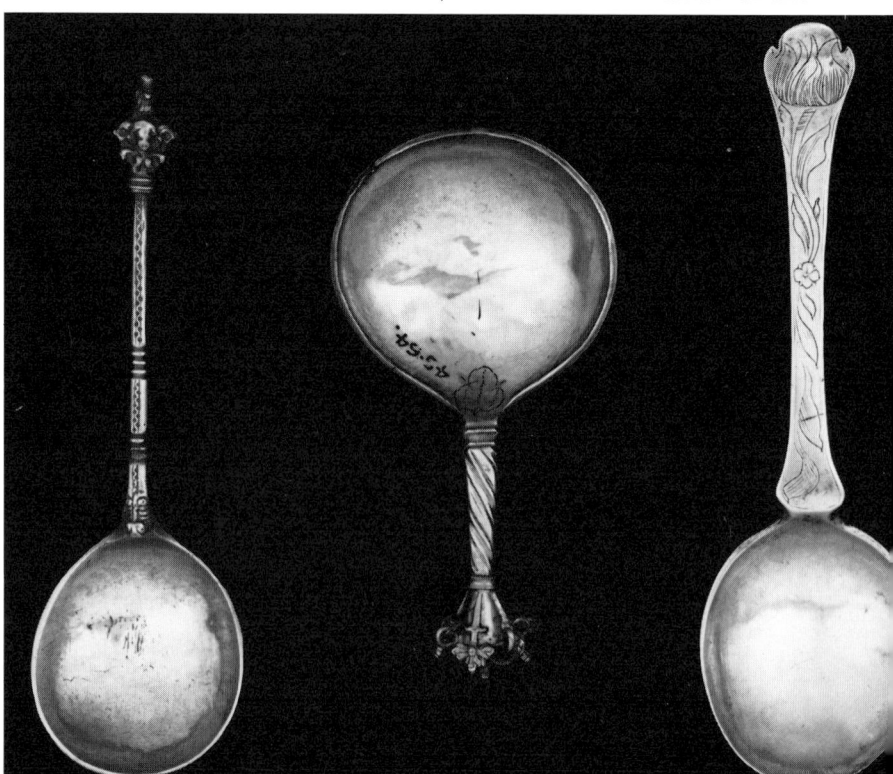

Scandinavian spoons made them awkward to handle. The stems were usually terminated by a cast head or a religious figure. These beautiful and interesting Gothic-style spoons of Scandinavia are very rare, even rarer than those produced in other countries.

At the end of the sixteenth century, the length of spoons increased to about 16 to 17 cm, when in other parts of the world they were reaching some 21 to 22 cm. The stems were of square or octagonal section, and the bowl became somewhat rounder. The stems terminated in a knop, in a manner already well-known in other countries and which persisted until the second half of the seventeenth century. Scandinavian silver spoons of the seventeenth century were in fact very similar to those made to the south, except in the detail of some of the tops, which might represent a bunch of grapes, a scallop shell, or cherubs' heads or female heads, back to back. Another finial used was the ball, but since ball spoons are found in other countries at about the same time, even in Belgium, a ball-knopped stem does not necessarily mean that the spoon was made in any of the Scandinavian countries. The Norwegians seem to be among the very rare craftsmen to have made stems with the lower part shaped as an oblong panel and the top as a twisted spiral, although some well-known Dutch spoons, such as a typical William and Mary spoon, made in silver and pewter, show the same characteristic. Collectors should be warned that many of the spoons made between the fifteenth and the seventeenth century were reproduced in Norway for the tourist trade during the nineteenth century. It is therefore not advisable to acquire such a spoon without having some knowledge of Scandinavian hallmarks.

Like other nations, the Scandinavians were bound to adopt the flat stem eventually, but they did it later than anywhere else. Spoons with knops and ornaments continued to be made for quite a long time, as they were very popular with the country people, but town dwellers wanted to follow the general European styles. The flat stems started to appear, slowly, during the second half of the seventeenth century, when the bowls became first circular then oval. But again there was a difference. Around the middle of the seventeenth century appeared a typical Scandinavian spoon, with an oval bowl and a flat stem terminated by a double rose, the stem itself decorated with engraved foliage. One peculiarity is that the stem had indented edges, a shape which is not recorded anywhere else in Europe. The well-known trefid spoon (or *pied de biche*) only reached Scandinavia at the very end of the seventeenth century, later than anywhere else, and many of them were made in silver and in brass. Some of the nicest examples are decorated with foliage motifs which are different from those found on French or British trefid spoons. The Scandinavians also adopted the dognose type in the eighteenth century, and it was followed around the middle of the century by the rounded-end spoon. The three types, trefid, dognose or rounded-end spoons, are sometimes very plain and carry no decoration at all, but all three can also be found decorated with typical Scandinavian motifs. Most of them have the characteristic decoration of two or three incised bands at the base of the stem, a motif sometimes repeated once or twice further up the stem. If that motif is encountered on spoons it is a clear indication that they are Scandinavian. Finally the fiddle-shaped stem was introduced during the second half of the eighteenth century, probably from models of Belgian or French origin. The fiddle-shaped spoons of Scandinavia are very similar to those found in France, with the fiddle shape clearly defined, but usually without the thread along the stem edges.

Then there are the Lapp spoons. For the people of Lapland, north of the Arctic Circle, now divided among four countries—Norway, Sweden, Finland and the USSR—were it seems as keen on silver spoons as their southern neighbours. But the spoons which Norwegian and Swedish silversmiths made for the Lapps were completely different from those made in the south, for they had to please their customers, and the Lapps had their own ideas and traditions, and their own folklore. They wanted spoons similar to those they carved themselves in elk horn, and the silversmiths therefore produced an astonishing range of spoons in silver, with short, wide, flat stems, and rounded or oval bowls, right from the start of the eighteenth century. Sometimes the stems carry seven, eight or nine hoops, with rings hanging from them. Sometimes holes were punched along the edges of the broad stems, again with rings attached. And most of these spoons are engraved with stylized flowers, zigzag borders and other traditional Lapp motifs. It is unlikely that such spoons could be found in the southern countries, but one never knows.

Above: Front and back of Russian gilt spoon, with handle in agathe decorated with turquoise stones (19th century); French electroplated silver tablespoon, after an 18th century model.

Below: Three early English silver spoons: unique "crest" maidenhead spoon (late 16th century); wrythen-knop spoon (mid 15th century); maidenhead spoon (London 1534). Courtesy Phillips Fine Art Auctioneers.

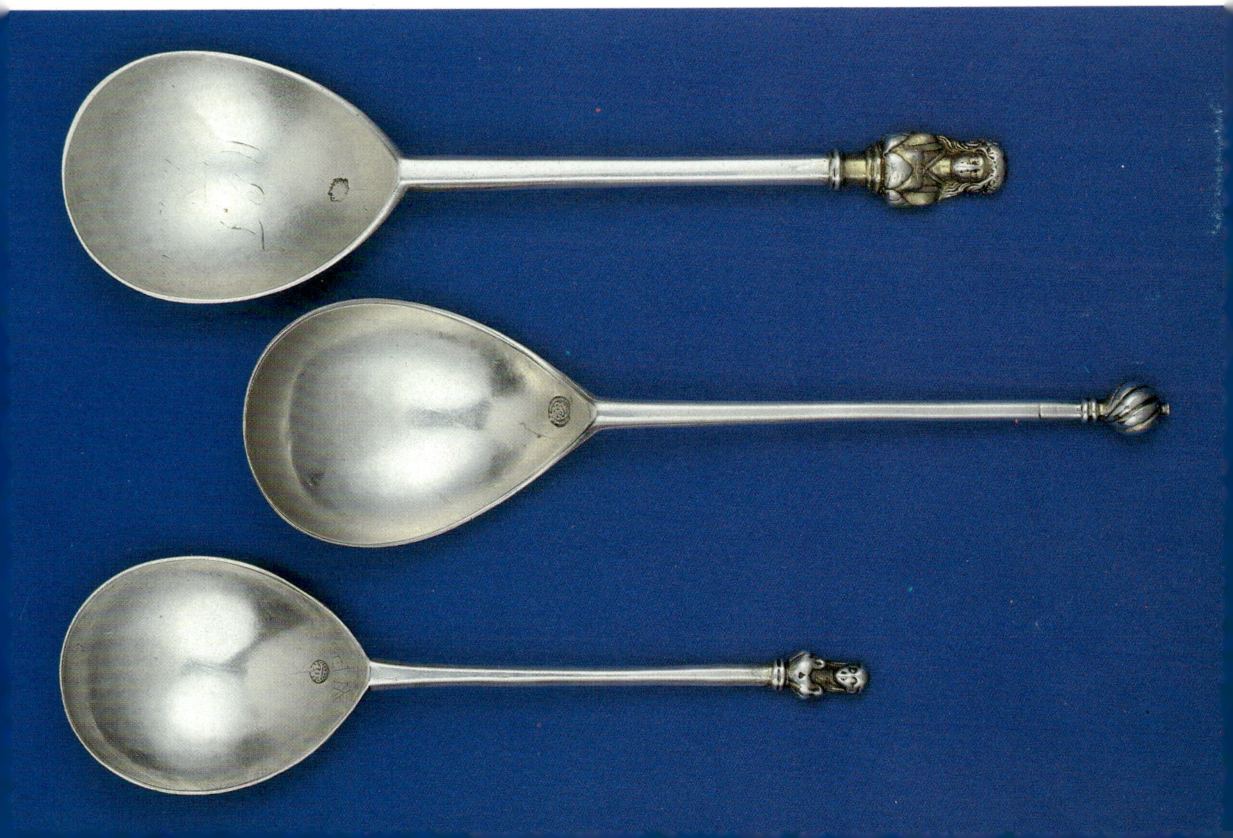

Above: Russian silver spoon terminated with the figure of a bear (Odessa). Coll. de Prins, Brussels.

Below, left to right: Trefid end spoon in brass (Sweden 18th century); Russian silver coffee spoon with caucasian design (1886–1908). Coll. de Prins, Brussels; Russian silver spoon decorated with architectural design in niello.

Above: Large Art Nouveau serving spoon in silver gilt (Germany, circa 1900)

Below: Six Russian enamel spoons (Moscow, 1886–1908). Coll. de Prins, Brussels.

Above, left to right: Dutch pewter spoon of the William and Mary type, often reproduced in Holland; Russian hand painted wooden spoon from Fedoskino; Russian silver spoon with back of bowl decorated with foliage motif in niello. (1865)

Below: Six Russian silver coffee spoons with bowls decorated with various architectural designs (Moscow 1872). Coll. de Prins, Brussels.

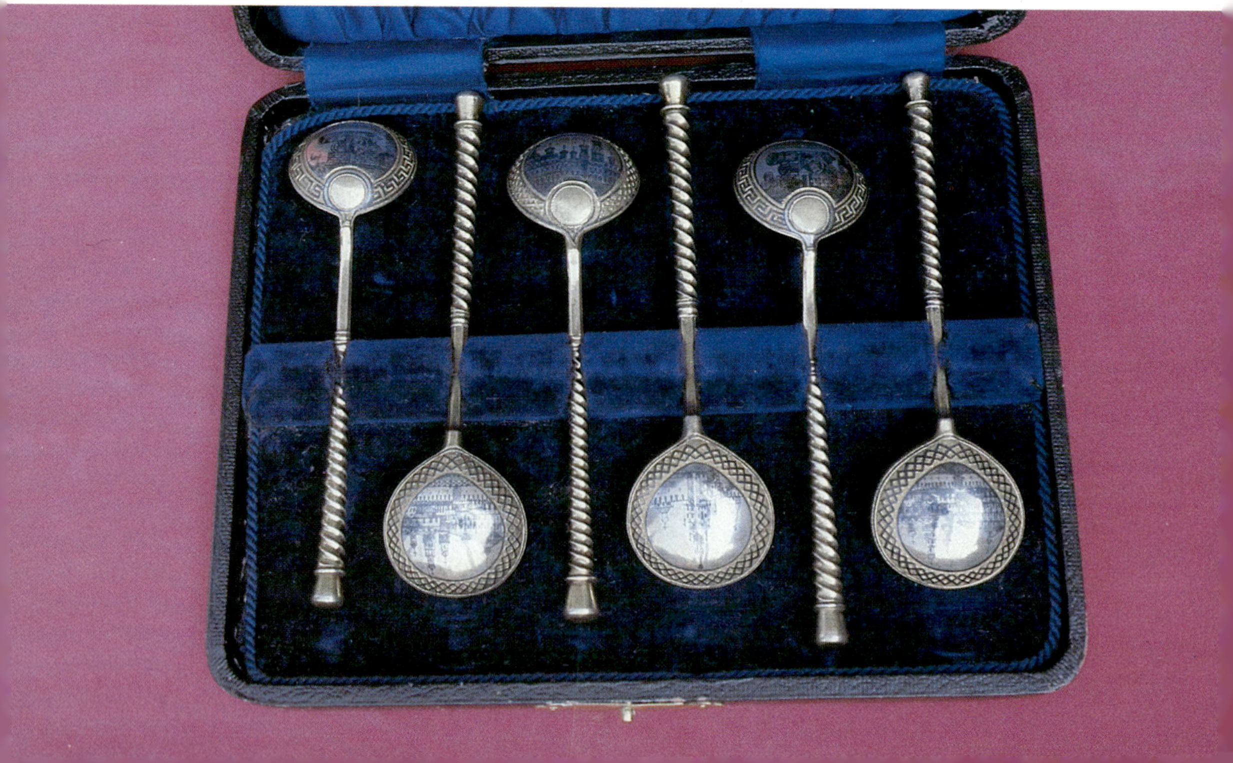

6 SPOONS OF THE SIXTEENTH AND SEVENTEENTH CENTURIES IN IVORY, HORN AND WOOD

W ooden spoons have always been made all over the world, from the very beginning of time, but they were never collected, being made of such a commonplace material. Instead they were thrown away or broken, and they have simply disappeared, leaving no trace. One is left to wonder what those wooden spoons were, which are mentioned so many times in wills and inventories, as if they had been made of gold or silver. They must have been very special to be mentioned in official documents. Thanks to a very ancient mediaeval document, the *Registre des métiers de Paris* (Register of Paris crafts), written about 1260, we know that Parisian spoonmakers were already very active at the time. The Register states, *'quilliers de boys . . . il ne doit point de tonlieu ni de coustume,'* implying that makers of wooden spoons did not have to pay taxes, and were free to make as many spoons as they liked. The *tonlieu* mentioned in the text was a tax that mediaeval dealers had to pay in order to have the right to sell their wares in fairs and markets. Spoonmakers were apparently exempt.

A very valuable Old French text of 1309 quoted by Victor Gay reveals how thirteenth- and fourteenth-century basting spoons were made. The text says: *'le zampe est un petit arbret . . . le bois en est bel et rouge et de grande oudeur et aucunement de plusiers couleurs; et ext tres bon pour faire bastes, pour ce qu'il donne a la chair sa bonne oudeur quand elle est rotie et aussi en faict-on de tres bonnes cuillers'* (the juniper is a small tree . . . its wood is nice and red and strong-smelling and of uniform colour; it is good to make *bastes*, for it gives the roasted meat its good taste, so it is used to make very good spoons). The word *baste* has lost all meaning in modern French, but it is probably cognate with the English verb 'to baste' and must have been applied to the stick of wood used to roast meat above an open fire and to the spoon used for basting. All the basting spoons known today are in silver or in other metals, and we can only lament the passing of those spoons made out of juniper wood, which apparently imparted such a delicious taste to the roasted meat.

Right from the beginning of the fourteenth century, spoons were made with wooden bowls and silver stems, and these too seem to have vanished for ever. French inventories and wills between the fourteenth and sixteenth centuries often refer to spoons '*a la turque*' or '*a la maniere des Sarrazins*', but the nature of these spoons in the Turkish or Saracen manner is a mystery. Does the name refer to a shape, a style, or what? The only certainty is that they were made of wood, and that they were also painted. The French royal inventory of 1400 includes a mention of 'two spoons in the Saracen manner, one white, one black'. The 1416 inventory of the famous Duke of Berry has 'two painted wooden spoons, in the Turkish manner'. These controversial spoons in wood went on being made for a very long time, for the will of one J. de Charmolue, written in 1599 and quoted by Victor Gay, contains the sentence: 'I leave to my cousin six spoons painted in the Turkish manner.' The only available clue is in the *Dictionnaire universel francais et latin*, otherwise known as the Trevoux dictionary, published in Paris in 1771; it states that 'spoons in the Turkish manner or spoons of the Turks are made of wood, with a stem as long as half a foot, which they used to prevent their fingers being burned.' The French foot was slightly longer than the present English foot, the equivalent of 33 cm, so Trevoux's Turkish spoon was 16·5 cm long, much the length of a modern spoon. Like various others we have mentioned, these spoons were probably of Eastern origin, and the model must have been brought back by returning Crusaders who had been in touch with the Turks. But as yet no one knows what they were used for, or what kind of designs were painted on them.

The great period of spoons made in ivory or wood belongs not to the Middle Ages but to the Renaissance, and the most magnificent extant examples were made during the sixteenth and seventeenth centuries, mainly in France, south Germany and Holland. Many of these carved masterpieces are now kept in museums and private collections, and now and then one appears in antique shops. In some ways they are better to look at than contemporary spoons made in silver or pewter. First, the figures which decorate them are larger than the usual figures found on silver specimens. Whereas a silver apostle for instance might be 2 cm tall, the same apostle in wood or ivory might be as much as 6 or 7 cm tall, and even taller when the figure itself constitutes the whole stem, as is sometimes the case.

The shapes and decorations of these ancient spoons are of such variety that a lifetime would not suffice to describe them all. And remember that most of those which were made have not come down to us. Dutch, German and French carvers excelled in this kind of artistic work, and produced real masterpieces in miniature. Some fine examples are the many apostle spoons delicately carved in boxwood, a favourite material. All kinds of wooden saint spoons are decorated with figures of saints not found in silver or in pewter, while the Virgin and Child often appear in wood or in ivory.

Two marvellous sets of carved spoons are now in the Deutsches Klingenmuseum of Sollingen (West Germany). The first is a complete set of ivory apostle spoons of the late sixteenth century, with the twelve apostles and the Master, still kept in their original tapering leather sheath. The second set, carved in boxwood and dating from the seventeenth century, consists of twelve spoons with stems decorated with figures of musicians, all different. Together they form a lovely miniature orchestra.

Certain wooden and ivory spoons, of the folding type, very rare on the market, are decorated with the figure of Christ on the Cross, a subject which does not exist in silver. One such extraordinary spoon from the sixteenth century is in the Germanisches Nationalmuseum, in Nuremberg. But it should be borne in mind that spoon stems, like knife handles, were not always decorated with carved Christian figures. Women, couples, all kinds of men, often unidentified, fruits,

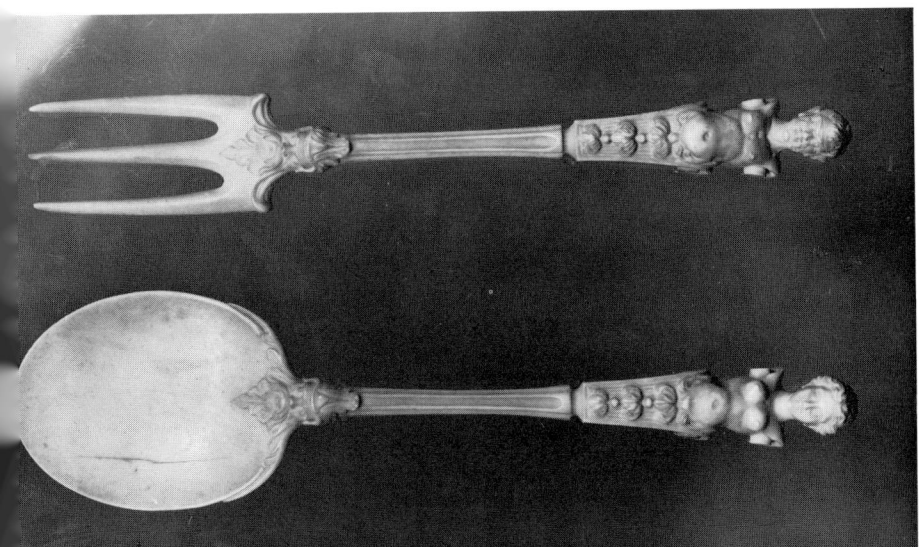

Beautiful and rare spoon and fork in ivory from the beginning of the 18th century. Probably French (?)
Musée Curtius Liege;
Copyright A.C.L.,
Brussels

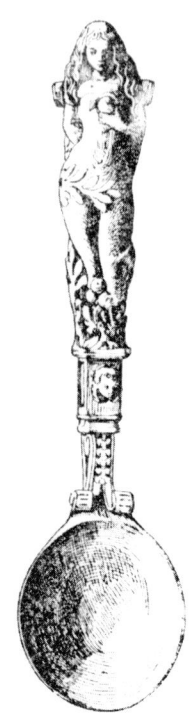

A rather extraordinary spoon, from the 16th century, carved out of one single piece of boxwood. The stem represents a naked woman holding her left breast in her left hand.

etc., were used as decorative motifs. The most sought-after, of course, are the pornographic ones, with women and men in all kinds of poses which can hardly be described. Most of the pornographic examples were made in Germany, and they always reach high prices.

One can get a faint idea of the variety of spoons in wood and ivory which were produced during the sixteenth and the seventeenth century by examining pictures of some of the spoons in the now vanished Figdor collection in Vienna, some of which were published by Henri d'Allemagne, himself the owner of an important collection. In the Figdor collection were some of the most typical spoons of the period, all of German origin, including a folding spoon with an oval bowl engraved with a simple cross and a finely carved boxwood stem portraying the Virgin and Child. The hinge of this seventeenth-century spoon is shaped as a console on which the Virgin is standing. Another folding spoon in the collection is carved out of a single piece of wood, a technical feat. The stem is terminated by a mobile acorn and is engraved 'Anno dei 1665'. The collection also had a sucket spoon and fork of the sixteenth century, in ivory. The spoon is of the folding type and has its bowl joined to the stem by a little carved mermaid who holds in her arms the cylinder containing the hinge axle. The stem itself, of square section, is decorated with flowers; its top is in the shape of a cube decorated with human faces and lions' heads, supporting a Corinthian capitol crowned by a figure of the Holy Virgin and Child.

In addition to the Holy Virgin so often represented on spoons in wood or ivory, a whole series of saints includes many not found on silver spoons. In the Figdor collection was a seventeenth-century folding spoon carved out of a single piece of boxwood, with a fig-shaped bowl. This spoon has a stem which is the figure of St Thomas, holding an axe in his right hand and a book in the other. Another carved boxwood spoon, of the early sixteenth century, has a twisted spiral stem terminated by the figure of St Bernard, who is holding a model church in his left arm and a small barrel in the other. One of the finest pieces in the collection was a seventeenth-century boxwood spoon decorated on top of the stem by the figure of St Joseph holding the Child in his left arm. The stem itself is decorated with vines and grapes. The figure of St Joseph holding the Child is

68

very rare in Christian iconography. This unique spoon has an angel's head carved at the feet of St Joseph, and this head has the particularity of being moveable to reveal a small cavity containing an ivory crucifix, so small that one needs the help of a magnifying glass to be able to appreciate the artistic skill of the carver.

The Figdor collection also had a horn spoon of the sixteenth century with a rather unusual stem for the period. It is straight, but flattened, with the figure of an armoured warrior on top. The warrior, who represents St Florian, holds a folded flag in his right hand. In his other hand he holds a vase from which he pours water on to a model church carved at his feet.

Every one of the spoons made in ivory or wood is practically unique. They can be decorated with the most unusual figures—half-clad Greek women, Leda and the Swan, St Catherine, naked children, all kinds of allegorical figures such as Justice or Charity, or lions' heads. One late sixteenth-century French example in the Bodo Glaub collection has a stem terminating in the figure of King Henri III of France. Many of those spoons in wood and ivory of the sixteenth and seventeenth centuries were in fact love spoons (see Chapter 9), like one published by Victor Gay in his *Glossaire d'archéologie du Moyen Age et de la Rennaissance*, which has a perfect oval bowl, in spite of having been made in France during the fifteenth century. The stem of this wooden spoon is carved in the likeness of an almost naked woman who clasps her left breast in her left hand. The reverse of the bowl is inscribed '*De Coeur, je le done*'; the meaning of this is not very clear.

It seems that the imagination of the sixteenth- and seventeenth-century carvers of wood and ivory knew no bounds, while at the same time the imaginative powers of the silversmiths were limited by the number of decent moulds they had at their disposal. Carving figures out of small pieces of wood or ivory was a difficult proposition, but on the other hand it gave artists complete freedom of interpretation, so that their lovingly worked spoons are real masterpieces in miniature. Some of them are also fully dated. Yet for some reason they are not collected as much as the silver examples of the same period, even though a collection of ivory spoons, for instance, constitutes a display fit for the most stately home or the most discerning museum.

7 SPOONS OF THE SEVENTEENTH CENTURY: THE AGE OF TRANSITION

Practically all the types of spoon which had been fashionable during the fifteenth and sixteenth centuries went on being made until well into the seventeenth century, both in Britain and on the Continent, with only a few exceptions. Apostle or saint spoons, hoof spoons, fist spoons, lion sejeant spoons, seal-top spoons, slip-top spoons and many others, including folding spoons, were produced during the first half of the century. Those seventeenth-century spoons made according to earlier models cannot be considered by collectors as copies at all: all of them are of great quality, and after all they are 300 years old.

It is among the spoons of the older types, but produced during the seventeenth century, that there is still a good chance of picking up a bargain. The fifteenth- and sixteenth-century examples are very rare, and beyond the reach of the average collector—unless of course he lives on the Continent, where dealers have a slight tendency to disdain spoons. Of course it may happen that some seventeenth-century copies of earlier types are not as good as the earlier models, for the simple reason that pewterers and silversmiths kept using the old moulds, and the wear and tear of many years sometimes shows on seventeenth-century spoons of the knop type.

However, one small technical change occurred at the very end of the sixteenth century which is of interest to spoon collectors. It was around 1590 that stems became longer than they had been previously, although the spoons still retained their fig- or pear-shaped bowls. This lengthening of the stems was the result of a change in dress fashion. Women and men had started wearing the big and awkward lace collars known as 'ruffles', very unpractical when it came to eating. Longer stems therefore became necessary, and spoons from the end of the sixteenth century often measured as much as 21 and even 22 cm, so that fashionable people could take

soup to their mouth without crumpling their ruff. It was no longer possible to use porringers for drinking soup, as had previously been the custom. Spoons were the thing.

One should remember that even at the beginning of the seventeenth century some very important people did not always appreciate spoons, or even forks. It is only then, and only in certain enlightened and wealthy circles, that forks and spoons began to be used at table. The adoption of these two utensils took some time, and even in 1650 persons as exalted as Anne of Austria, Queen of France, were still using their fingers to eat. It was not till the last quarter of the century that the use of forks and spoons at table became a general

Beautiful French trefid spoon dated 1681. *Courtesy Victoria and Albert Museum, London*

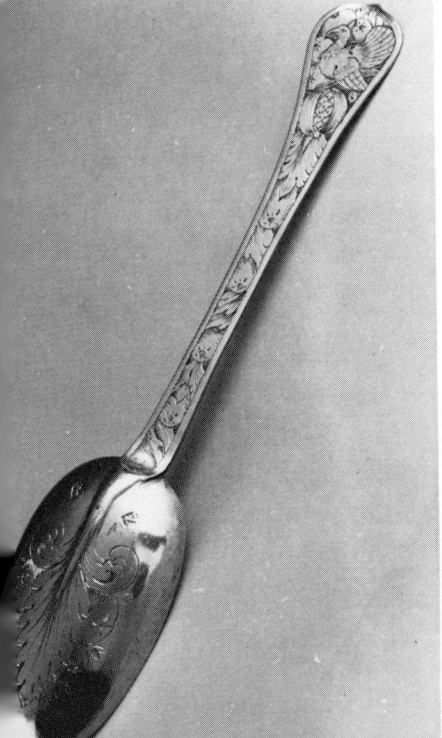

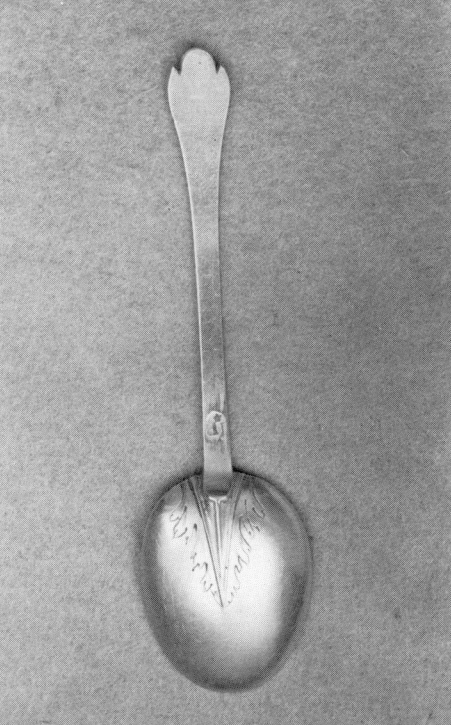

Left: Beautifully decorated silver Swiss spoon from the 17th century. Zurich hallmark, length 17.9 cm. *Copyright A.C.L., Brussels*

Right: Gold trefid spoon made by John Phillips of Dublin, circa 1680. Only two other gold table spoons from the period are known to be in existence. *Courtesy Worshipful Company of Goldsmiths, London*

practice in most households. This is also the period when big serving spoons were introduced.

The French writer Saint-Simon, reporter *par excellence* on the court of France in the seventeenth century, explains that: 'Monsieur de Montpensier, who lived in great splendour, was terrible at the table and had been the inventor of big spoons and big forks, which became fashionable.' It is doubtful if Monsieur de Montpensier invented anything of the kind. The habit of using big serving spoons also led to some comic incidents, as people sitting round the table did not always know what they were for. The French writer La Bruyere told of one such incident in his *Characteres*, Chapter XI: 'Big spoons have been invented for serving at table. Menalchas takes it, dips it in a dish, fills it, takes it to his mouth and is amazed to see that the soup he is supposed to eat is spread all over him.' These big serving spoons crop up in the French crown inventory, dated 20 February 1673: 'three spoons with long stems to serve stews and sweets, in silver gilt'.

A reading of contemporary documents more or less establishes that large serving spoons were introduced around the mid-seventeenth century into practically all European countries. It was roughly during the same period that new, more practical and simpler spoons replaced the old-fashioned spoons of Gothic inspiration, most of which gradually fell into disuse (with certain exceptions, like the apostle spoon). But collectors should be careful, for later examples of these antique spoons might just be fakes, made to deceive. In his book *Oude Zilveren Lepels*, E. M. C. F. Klijn, who only examined the spoons now in the collections of the Arnhem Open Air Museum, gives a clear warning to collectors, mainly to the British

A spoon, fork and knife, with carved ivory handles with intertwined putti and cherubs. The silver spoon bowl is engraved with stylised foliage. Dutch, 17th century. *Courtesy Sotheby Parke Bernet & Co., London*

collectors. According to him, many fakes were made in Holland at the turn of the century for export to England.

By the middle of the seventeenth century the age of transition had been reached, and new types of spoon were needed on all tables. Silversmiths and pewterers started to make the real ancestors of our modern spoons. A very special type of spoon made from the beginning of the century is the sucket spoon, now very rare and much sought after by collectors. The sucket spoon-and-fork set was made for the use of travellers. They existed before the start of the seventeenth century, but in very small numbers, and they were of two different types. The first and simpler type, found practically exclusively in Britian, is designed with a small rat-tailed spoon bowl at one end and a two-pronged fork at the other end of the usually square-section stem. This first type might have been useful in certain circumstances, but not for travelling. Most of the extant examples of this spoon, like a spoon now in the Exeter Museum, come from the seventeenth century; proof of their presence in the previous century is an entry in the inventory of King Edward VI, written in 1549: 'item one suckett spone wt a fork joyned together of silver gylte'. The later versions of this British spoon and fork are sturdier than the earlier examples, and some are even equipped with a three-pronged fork. These spoons are rather small, averaging 13 cm in length, and the earlier examples had circular, not to say nearly spherical bowls which become more and more oval as the century draws to its close.

Another type of sucket spoon and fork, a few of which were also produced as early as the sixteenth century, is found on the Continent, mainly in France, Germany and the Low Countries. It consists of a two- or three-pronged fork and a separate spoon bowl equipped with two or three bolts through which the fork prongs could be passed, thereby securing the bowl to the stem. The most magnificent example of this type of spoon was in the Albert Figdor collection in Vienna. No one knows its present whereabouts, but it is described and illustrated in *Accessoires du Costume et de la Décoration* by Henri d'Allemagne, who himself had a fine collection of antique spoons. It is the St George spoon, manufactured in Germany in the first half of the sixteenth century. Unlike the other examples, this spoon is in three parts, all in silver gilt. The finial of the fork represents the figure of a man in the attitude of prayer, with hands

A Dutch silver folding spoon, circa 1600, beautifully engraved, with a knop representing a goat's head. *Courtesy Victoria and Albert Museum, London*

73

joined together. This finial can be unscrewed, revealing a pen hidden in the stem. The second part is the fork handle itself, decorated on one side with the figure of St George killing a dragon and on the other side with the caryatid of a man terminated in a scroll. On the sides of the fork handle are attached a toothpick and an earpick. The oval bowl itself forms the third part of this curiosity. It is decorated on top of the reverse with another caryatid, this time of a woman. It is not immediately obvious why it should have an earpick attached to it, or for that matter the pen hidden in the stem. But it shows that the sucket spoon and fork really was a travelling model.

The sucket spoon and fork met with great success in Germany and the Low Countries. The Brussels Museum has two spoons of this type, in silver, both equipped with a three-pronged fork and a stem which can be unfolded and then held in place when eating by a sliding ring. There is an angel's head at the joint between stem and fork. To make them more interesting, the finials of the stems are decorated with the figure of an ancient warrior. Although those two sucket spoons and forks are identical, one was made in Antwerp in 1663, the other, also in Antwerp, in 1674–5, an indication that this type of utensil retained its popularity. The later of these two spoons still has its leather sheath, decorated with golden motifs. In fact it seems probably that these sucket spoons and forks were always sold in a sheath, but in many cases they have disappeared.

Sucket spoons and forks, very interesting articles to collect, were made until the eighteenth century, when in fact it was quite unnecessary to carry one's own fork and spoon. The Bodo Glaub collection in Cologne has a sucket fork and spoon similar to the Brussels pair, in silver, with a lion sejant on top of the stem, attributed to the first half of the eighteenth century, with a pear-shaped bowl and a folding fork stem. A second sucket spoon and fork in the same collection, also in silver, from the first quarter of the seventeenth century, has the usual pear-shaped bowl, but the stem

74

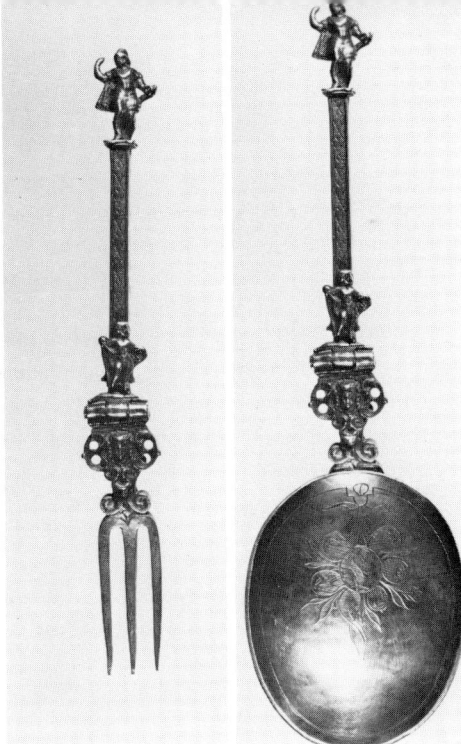

of the fork is terminated by a disc, in the manner of the Scottish disc-end spoons. In both cases the forks are three-pronged.

As already mentioned, most of the Gothic-inspired spoons were made during the first half of the seventeenth century, including spoons of the luxury type. Yet the days of such extravagance were really over. During the second half of the century, Charles Perrault, the French author of so many world-famous fairy stories, could still write in his *Sleeping Beauty*: 'Before each one of them was a magnificent sheath of solid gold in which were a spoon, a fork and a knife, also in gold, decorated with diamonds and rubies,' but of course it was a fairy story. The spoon as a luxurious objet d'art was a thing of the past.

Gradually the spoon became a very normal and everyday table utensil, which did not have to be fancy but practical, and as cheap as possible. The transition had already started when more people used the simple slip-top spoon, the successor of the cut-end spoon of the Middle Ages. For the beautiful spoons one would like to collect today were made for a very small proportion of people. The poor and the not so rich could not afford to buy them and had to content themselves, if not with wooden spoons, then with much simpler and cheaper models in pewter or brass. The cut-end spoons of the Middle Ages gave way in the fifteenth century to the only slightly fancier slip-top spoons, which went on being made until around 1660. Both types were mainly made in pewter.

Around 1640, a new type replaced the slip-top spoon. This, the 'puritan' spoon, marked a great change. It had a particularly flat stem, though quite heavy in fact, and a knopless tip. The end of the spoon was cut at right-angles, while the bowl became egg-shaped or oval. On some extant examples the square top is sometimes broken by one or two notches, which were not functional. The great idea was to flatten the stem, or at least to make it wider than the previous straight stems of square, hexagonal or octagonal section. Previous spoons had not been very practical to use, as it was rather difficult to hold them in one's hand. To realize the difficulty, collectors should

Sucket spoon and fork in silver. The finial represents an antique warrior, and the inside of the bowl is engraved with a bowl of fruit. Antwerp 1674. *Copyright A.C.L., Brussels*

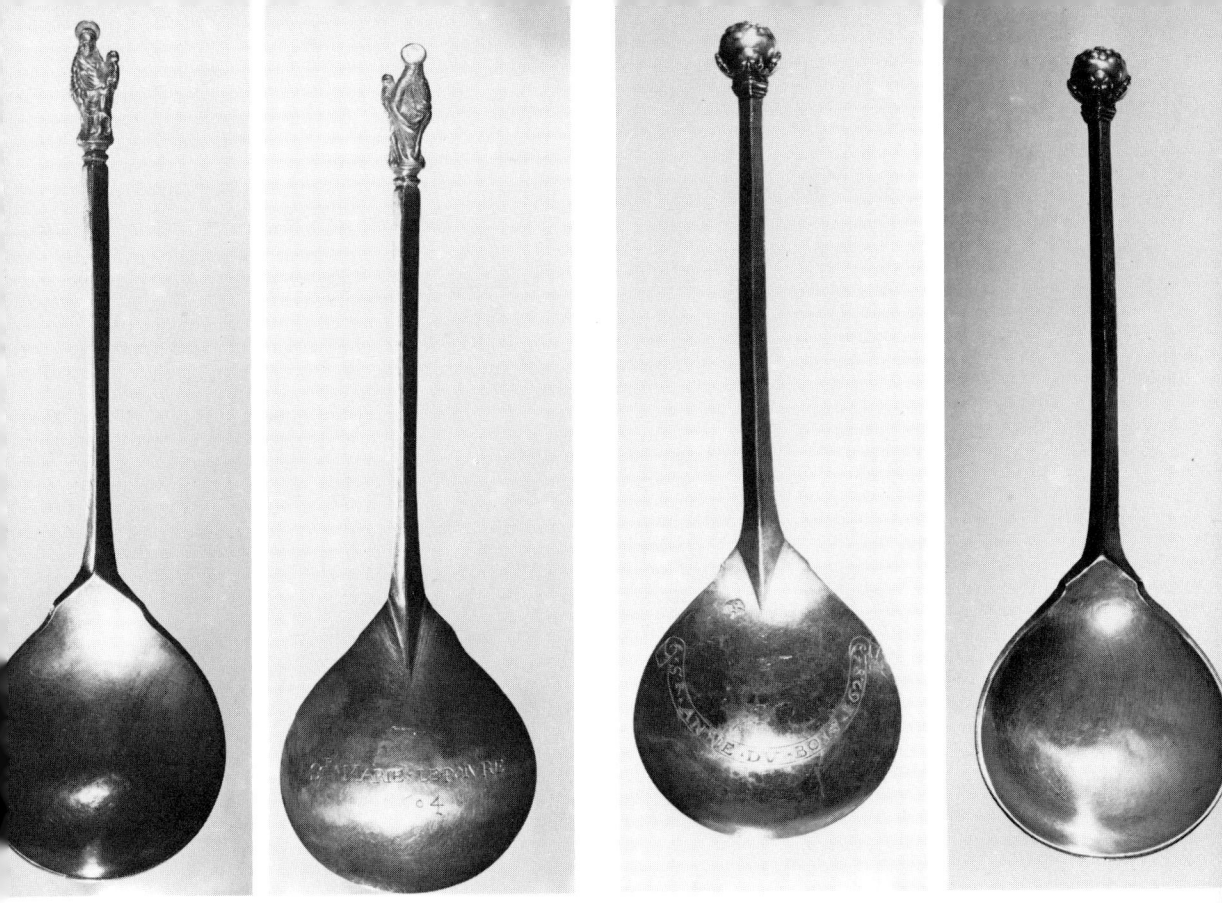

Left: Virgin and child silver spoon, unmarked, probably Flemish. The reverse of the bowl is engraved 'Sr Marie le Poivre' above the date 1604. *Copyright A.C.L., Brussels*

Right: Silver spoon with rounded fig-shaped bowl and square section stem, from the beginning of the 17th century. The finial represents a raspberry on four small leaves. The reverse of the bowl is decorated with the inscription 'Sr Anne du Bois – 1628'. Hallmark AR, but no town mark. Southern Netherlands. *Copyright A.C.L., Brussels*

try to eat soup with a spoon equipped with a round stem. Now for the first time you could hold your spoon firmly in your hand.

It was also during this period that fig-shaped bowls were replaced or rather superseded by the egg-shaped or oval bowl, another improvement.

At the same time there appeared the next in the line of evolution, the trefid spoon, otherwise known by its French name of *'pied de biche'* (hind's foot). The type originated in France, and was well established there in the mid-seventeenth century. It was the main style of spoon in France during the reign of Louis XIV, the Sun King, which lasted from 1643 until 1715. The *pied de biche* was adopted immediately by the Low Countries, and some years later, around

Left: Folding spoon from the 17th century, the inside of the bowl engraved with a bunch of fruits with foliage. The finial is composed of an antique warrior, often found on folding spoons, made in Antwerp in the second half of the 17th century. Unmarked. *Copyright A.C.L., Brussels*

Right: Flemish brass spoon from the first quarter of the 17th century, the finial composed of two unidentified figures, probably lovers. *Copyright A.C.L., Brussels*

1660, by the British. Louis XIV himself used pied de biche spoons, in gold and engraved on the spatula or spatulate end with the arms of France.

The trefid spoon or *pied de biche*, which continued to be made until well into the eighteenth century in every country of Europe, including Scandinavia, is easy to recognize because it has a very flat stem, broader at the end, with the tip divided by two clefts. It is slightly turned up at the end, and the bowl is oval and reinforced at the back by a rat-tail, a type of attachment already known by the Romans. Some trefid spoons were made in silver, but most were in pewter or brass. Of the very few extant examples in gold, one is dated *c* 1680 and belongs to the Worshipful Company of Goldsmiths.

The trefid style remained more or less fashionable in France, Britain and a few other countries for a good half-century. No matter where they were made, they often had their stems decorated with scrollwork or foliage. About thirty years after the introduction of the trefid spoon into Britain, the notches at the end of the stem were omitted, thus leading to the creation of the so-called 'dognose' spoon, hardly a real improvement. (The end of the stem now looked rather like the profile of a dog's head seen from above.) The style was also adopted on the Continent, and it remained fashionable until the end of Queen Anne's reign, which coincided with the end of Louis XIV's. A few rare dognose spoons were made in silver or gold, but mostly they were in pewter, and sometimes in brass.

Another style which was invented by the French and became very popular on the Continent was the fiddle pattern spoon, which had the end of its stem shaped exactly like the profile of a fiddle. It was immediately adopted by the Germans, the Dutch and the southern

A quite rare James I moor's head spoon, by Daniel Cary, London 1620. *Courtesy of Phillips, London*

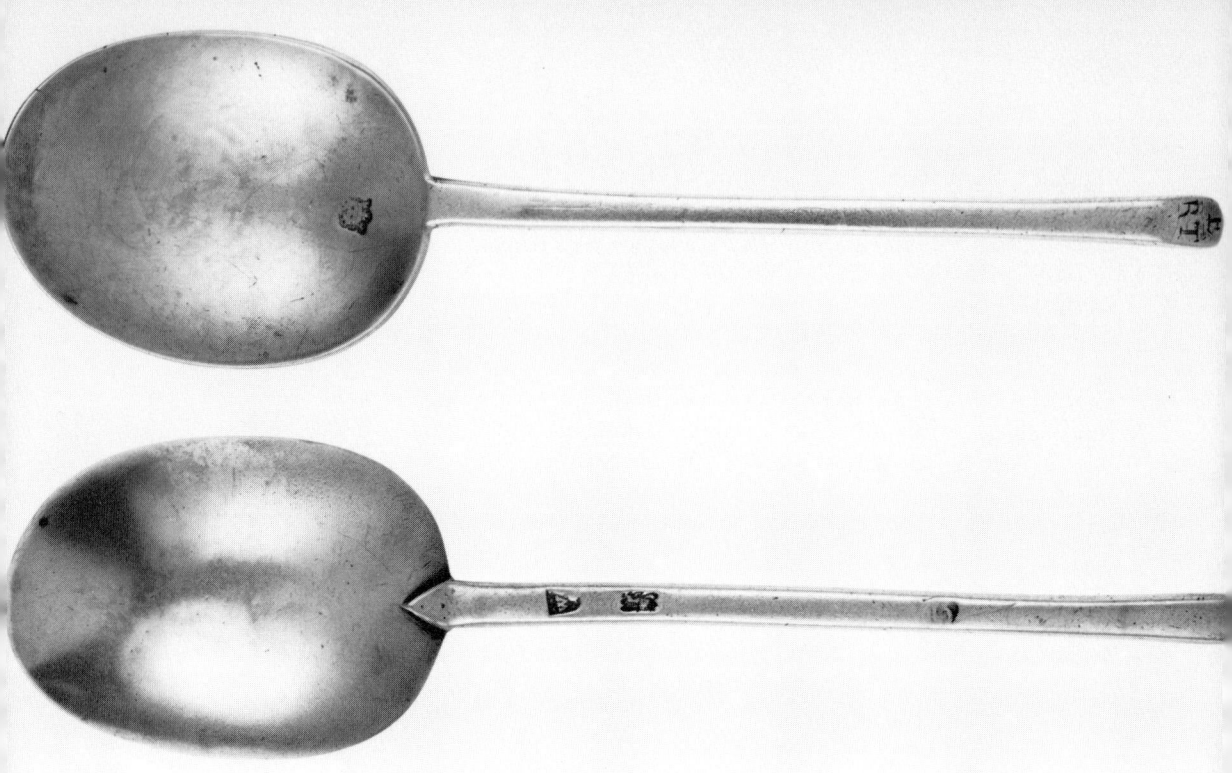

Back and front views of puritan spoon by William Cary, dated 1653. *Courtesy of Phillips, London*

Low Countries at the turn of the century, and many early eighteenth-century examples are still extant. The true continental fiddle pattern was never adopted by the British all through the eighteenth century, but they gave the name of fiddle pattern to a subsequent style developed in France around 1725, where the end of the stem became a near perfect oblong (a spatulate end). The name 'fiddle pattern' applied to this late style has been thought quite inappropriate by many in Britain, and quite logically, for the oblong shape has no resemblance to the shape of a fiddle.

But apart from the stem, the spoon in itself had hardly changed. During the first quarter of the eighteenth century only, the bowl became narrower and elliptical, always with a rat-tail down the back

Right: Fine silver puritan spoons by unidentified London and provincial masters. From left to right: maker's mark 'IG', London, circa 1660; maker's mark, 'SV', provincial, second half of the 17th century; maker's mark initials R and W above each other, provincial, second half of the 17th century; maker's mark 'AG', provincial, circa 1675; maker's mark the initials R and H conjoined, maybe Leicester, circa 1675. *Courtesy of Phillips, London*

80

of the bowl, and—great innovation—the stem end which had always been turned down was turned up instead. The real modern form was to be created during the middle of the eighteenth century, when the top of the bowl became narrower than the base and the stem end rounded.

It was at the end of the seventeenth century, however, that dinner services were produced for the first time, though only for the benefit of the very rich. France once more led the way, and tables were properly set before people sitting at the table. There was no question of using those magnificent folding knives, spoons and forks. People had only to sit down and use the flatware laid on the table in front of them. There were identical plates, identical forks, identical knives, identical spoons. The French court of Louis XIV set the example to all of Europe, for the Sun King had many such dinner sets, including some that he took with him every time he went campaigning somewhere. From France the custom spread to all the European courts, from Sweden to Holy Russia, the German courts, in fact everywhere. And they all ordered their dinner services from Paris. Louis XIV, the man who wore diamond buttons on his clothes, used gold spoons, gold forks, gold knives.

If seventeenth-century services are rare, the eighteenth-century adopted the idea with enthusiasm, and private persons who could afford such luxury ordered their own dinner services, mostly in silver. Louis XV insisted on being served as royally as his predecessor on the throne, and some superb rococo services were supplied by the Parisian silversmiths to foreign customers, while simpler services, still very beautiful, were ordered from Germany, mainly from Augsburg. In the matter of dinner services, the British were some way behind the French, and the first services were not made there until the beginning of the eighteenth century. The story goes that many ambassadors were supplied with dinner services to take abroad with them. But dinner services, once invented, were here to stay and they were starting to become common all over Europe by the middle of the eighteenth century, with spoons following the fashion of the time—fiddle-shaped, dognose, trefid end, spatulate end, all the fashionable styles. Most of the late eighteenth-century spoons found today, and they are not as rare as they are often supposed to be, belonged to dinner services.

8 SPOONS OF THE EIGHTEENTH CENTURY

At the very end of the seventeenth century, the spoon was definitely accepted and used as a normal table utensil by people of all social categories, all over Europe. It was during the next fifty years or so that the modern spoon, the one we use every day, started to take its shape, which was to remain practically unchanged ever after. And this is logical enough, when you start thinking about it. The spoon is functional: it is made to pick up food the easiest way. It has to be easy to hold, and it has to take food from plate to mouth without spilling—a risk which was always there with the old spoons with their narrow straight stems. The food however has not changed, and the morphology of the human being has not changed. Trial and error eventually produced an established shape, and that was that.

The pied de biche spoon, adopted everywhere and introduced into Britain around 1660, is the type which a few years later was to lead to the modern spoon. It was not developed from the puritan spoon, as it was first made in France, where the puritan spoon was unknown. The puritan spoon was rather bowl-heavy, and not so easy to handle, whereas the trefid spoon was well balanced and more elegant to look at. The lovely trefid spoon, which was made in silver, in pewter and in brass, was slightly modified at the end of the seventeenth century when the two notches at the top of the stem were simply removed, leading to the new dognose pattern. Of course the oval bowl which is found on most trefid spoons was gradually elongated. It was in fact the basic design of the modern spoon. The dognose design, rather unusual but adopted practically everywhere, was finally rounded off somewhere around 1715 or so, but spoonmakers remained faithful to the ancient rat-tail attachment for another few years, in some cases up to the second half of the eighteenth century.

An early 18th century trefid spoon with lace back bowl and terminal pricked 1704 below the initials I.S.P., by Edward Sweet of Dunster, circa 1700. *Courtesy Sotheby Parke Bernet & Co., London*

83

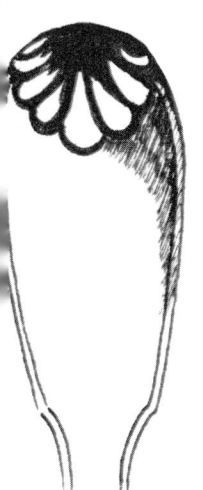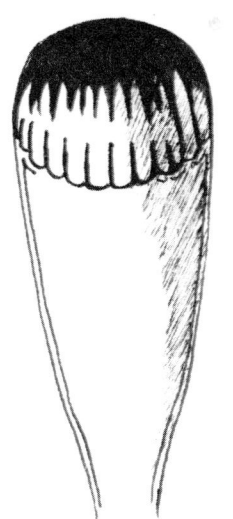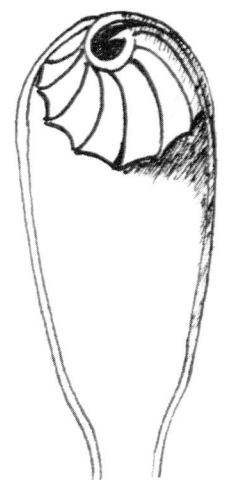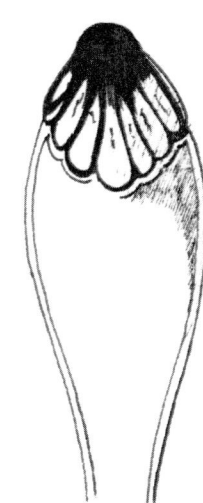

Towards the end of Louis XIV's reign, and therefore of the Queen Anne period, the end of the stem was slightly turned up. And then, but gradually, the rat-tail attachment found on so many antique spoons began to be replaced by a shorter attachment, known as the single or double drop. What is amazing is the fact that these variations or improvements, whatever they are, were adopted in many countries at about the same time, as if the spoonmakers from various countries had kept in touch and exchanged information. The double drop is found in France, Belgium, Holland and other countries during the eighteenth century. It seems that before the adoption of this new device the spoonmakers first used a short triangle as attachment, still a reminder of the rat-tail, and then the triangle was rounded to become a drop.

Collectors should realize that it always takes some time for a new style to emerge. It is always a laborious process, and for many years two styles might just overlap. Spoonmakers did not suddenly, one day, decide to stop using the rat-tail and replace with a drop, which explains why some spoons of around 1715 might have a double drop attachment, while some others from the second half of the century might still have the rat-tail attachment. But whatever the likes and dislikes of spoonmakers, the round stem-end started to become fashionable at the beginning of the eighteenth century everywhere

Four different types of shells decorating French 18th-century spoons. The shell spoon was created at the very beginning of the century, but was in general use only, starting around 1720.

Left: Five spoons with dog-nose finial. Two on the left by Francis Archbold, London 1704. The middle one by Thomas Spackman, London, 1710. The fourth one by William Petley, London, 1709, and the last one by William Scarlett, London, 1704. *Courtesy of Phillips, London*

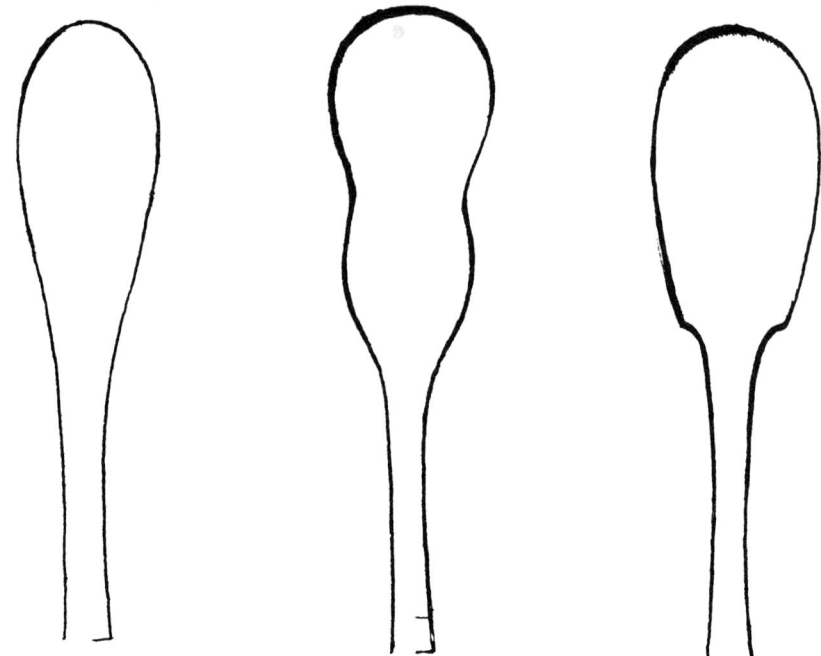

French 18th century Spoon Styles
Until about 1725, the spoons manufactured in France were copies of the old 17th-century styles, with very often the stem still attached to the bowl by means of a rat-tail. Starting in the second quarter of the 18th century, the rat-tail was replaced by a double knop, then by a single knop. The first and simplest spoon style was what is called 'the uni-plat', a spoon with a flat and straight stem tapering to form a 'spatula' rounded at the top and curving slightly downward. This 'uniplat' model has survived and is still made today. As far as the forms are concerned, only three patterns were made during the whole 18th century: the straight spatulated stem, inherited from the 17th century, the spatulated shouldered stem which appeared at the beginning of the century, and the violin or fiddle shape which was adopted around 1725.

in Europe. At a later date some authors, noticing that the new style coincided more or less with the accession to the English throne of George I, decided to call it the Hanoverian pattern, a name which is naturally not applied to spoons of similar style in other countries.

The late seventeenth-century English trefid spoons and the dognose spoons of the same period were simple, even severe, at first, and did not carry any kind of decoration. Then, at the very end of the century it seems, the severe surfaces of the stems started being decorated with scratch engravings. Such spoons, which are not too hard to find, carry all kinds of motifs such as mythological or fancy birds, various kinds of foliage, and very often acanthus motifs on the reverse of the bowl along the rat-tail terminal. Die-struck motifs of foliage decorated the front of the stems, making the spoons much

Three examples of French 18th-century fiddle-shaped spatula decorations. The three different types of shell decorating the top of the stems have been popular ever since with French spoonmakers.

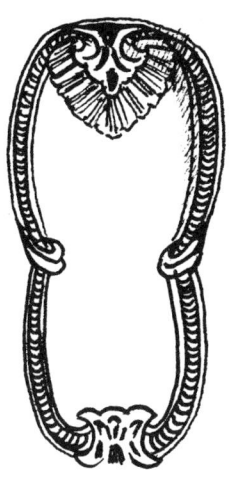

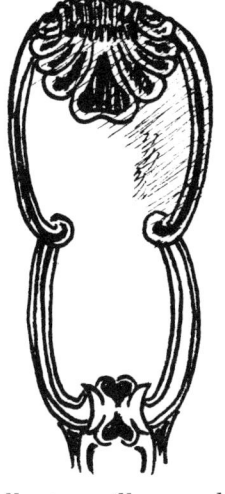

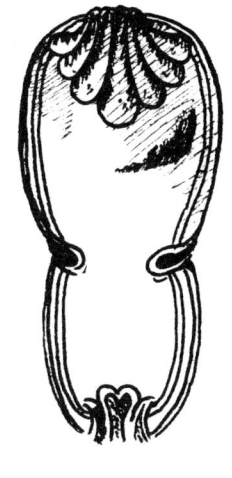

more decorative, and a collector will never hesitate between a trefid spoon bare of all decoration and the spoons of the same type carrying beautiful engravings. The trefid spoons of other countries such as France, Holland and Scandinavia were similarly engraved, and many carried initials, probably the owner's, on the larger part of the stem, near the top. These spoons are called lace-back in Britain; other countries where there is less collector interest have no special name for them.

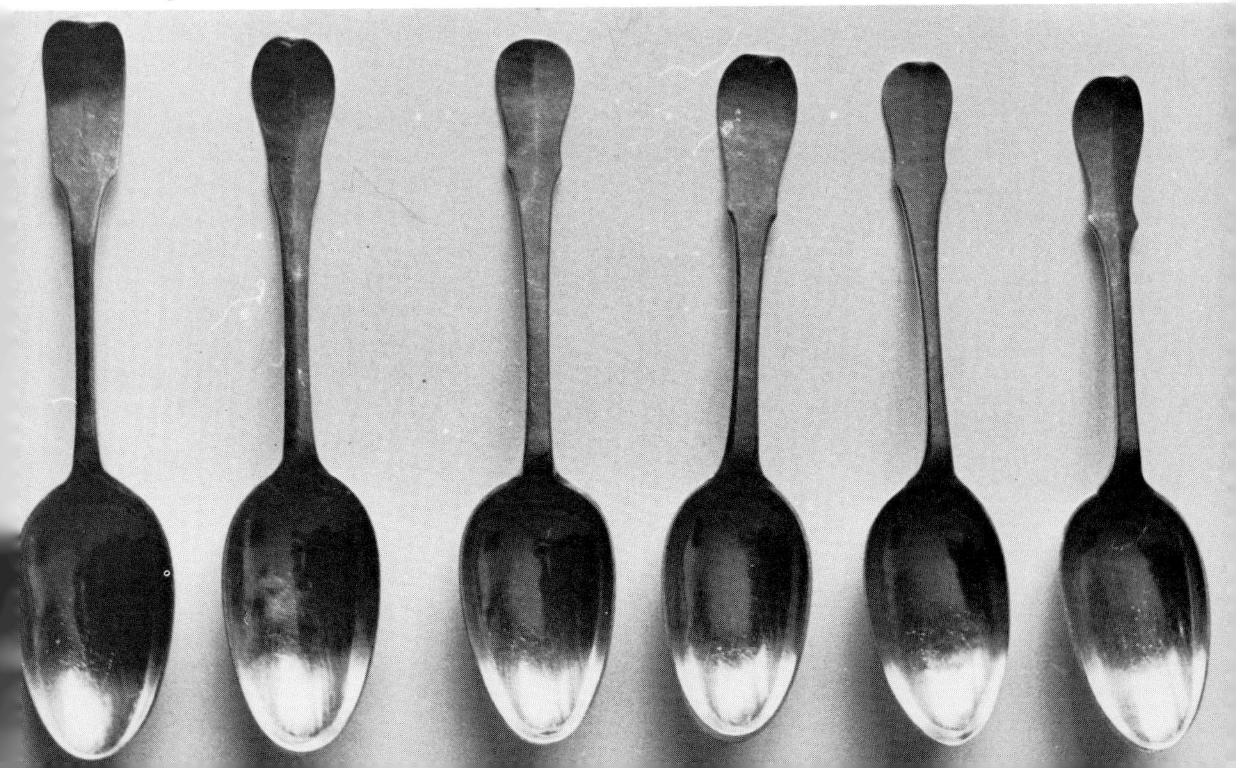

The Hanoverian pattern gave way in Britain, somewhere between 1740 and 1750, to the so-called English pattern, the only difference being that the end of the stem was turned down when before it had

Six various Belgian silver poons of the second half of the 18th century, each one bearing a different town mark. *Private collection*

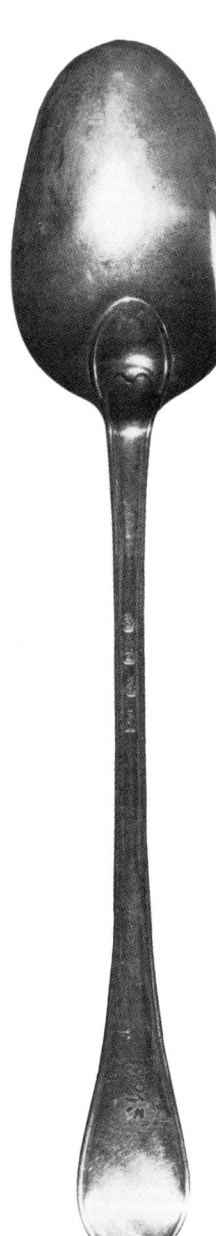

been turned up. The English pattern continued to be used in Britain throughout the nineteenth century, and in fact it is still used today. As a rule Hanoverian spoons and English pattern spoons are quite plain, but starting around the middle of the eighteenth century some spoonmakers started decorating them with engravings to justify the name fancy-back. Most of these decorated spoons are of small size, teaspoons and dessert spoons, decorated with all kinds of scrolls, shells and other ornamental designs in place of the double drop attachment, just below the junction of bowl to stem.

Fancy-back spoons were made in vast quantity until the end of the century, and even in the following century, and they provide a good opportunity to assemble a sizeable collection without undue difficulty. The reverse of the bowl is decorated with die-struck motifs of various inspiration, political or heraldic. Some are taken from the farmyard and animal kingdom, and all possible subjects are to be found on them—chickens, milkmaids, crossed rakes, wheatsheaves, dolphins, stags. The three feathers of the Prince of Wales are well known, as are double-headed eagles and baskets of flowers. Masonic emblems are extremely rare and much sought after. The motifs are so various that one could not possibly list a quarter of them. These fancy-back spoons are very British of course, but some spoons of similar type were also made on the Continent.

The continental spoons of the eighteenth century are somewhat different, and their evolution took other paths, most of them inspired by French, and in particular Parisian, silversmiths. The extant French material is very fragmentary, but two distinct types of French silver spoons can be identified: on one side a very courtly art, of the highest technical refinement; on the other a most utilitarian art, very simple in workmanship. The French, soon followed by other nationalities, started producing trefid-end spoons quite a few years before the British did, and these seventeenth-century trefid spoons were decorated with scratch engravings of foliate motifs, a type of ornamentation which was adopted by other countries a few years later. The trefid style remained in favour in France all during the Louis XIV period, and was followed by the dognose pattern, but

Typical 18th-century spoon with thread and teardrop, oval bowl and double knop attachment. *Copyright A.C.L., Brussels*

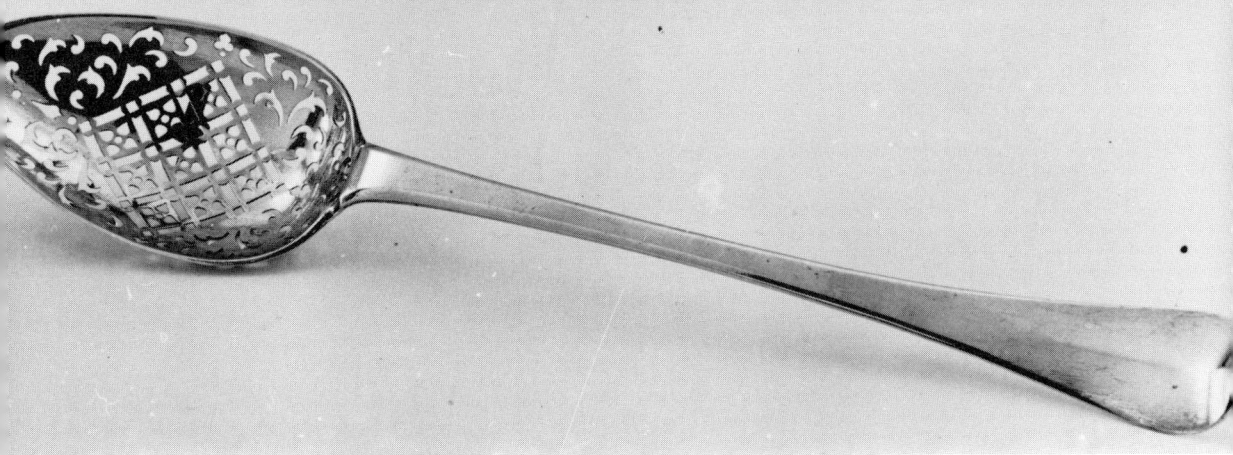

this never achieved the popularity it enjoyed in Britain, although some lovely dognose pattern spoons are to be found in some of the many dinner services that the Sun King owned.

Very early in the eighteenth century, following the dognose pattern, another more beautiful style, the fiddle pattern, took hold. Silver and pewter spoons of this pattern had already appeared in France right at the end of the seventeenth century, and the idea spread rapidly to neighbouring countries, notably to the Low Countries, where silversmiths continued to produce spoons of that pattern until the very end of the eighteenth century. It was of course the real fiddle pattern, with the end part of the stem shaped like the profile of the violin, hence its French name, *forme violon*. The fiddle shape was also adopted by the French pewterers at the end of the seventeenth century, and some beautiful pewter spoons can be found in the Musée des Arts Decoratifs in Paris. They have a typical fiddle pattern, an elongated bowl, and a depressed line following the contours of the stem, an element which is also found on French silver spoons at the end of the seventeenth century. This depressed line was to lead some years later to a narrow moulded border called a thread or double thread, a type of ornamentation which was adopted much later in Britain, at the same time as the misnamed British 'fiddle pattern' whose stem is not shaped like a fiddle.

Another pattern found in France in the early eighteenth century was the shell type. The shell motif was used on spoons for the simple reason that the cockle-shell was one of the decorative elements of the

Olive spoon in silver, from the 18th century. Hallmark of Tours, France. *Copyright A.C.L., Brussels*

A French Louis XV spoon from the middle of the 18th century, which shows the violin-shaped stem, with a shell terminating in what the French call a 'lip' on top of the shell. It also shows the shoulder attachment of stem to bowl.

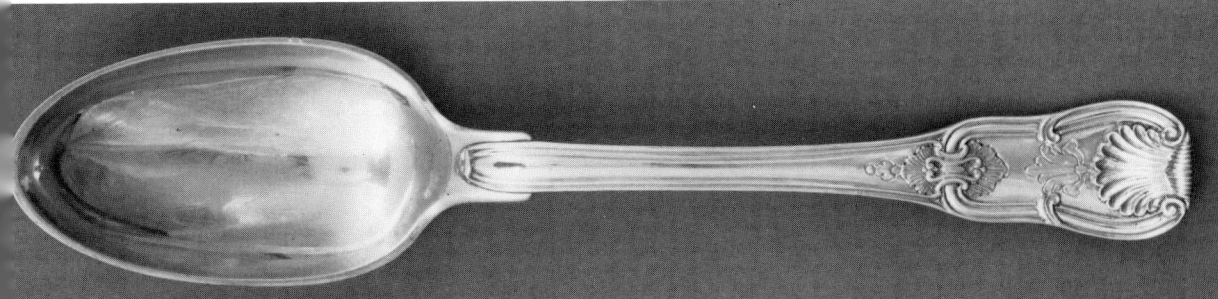

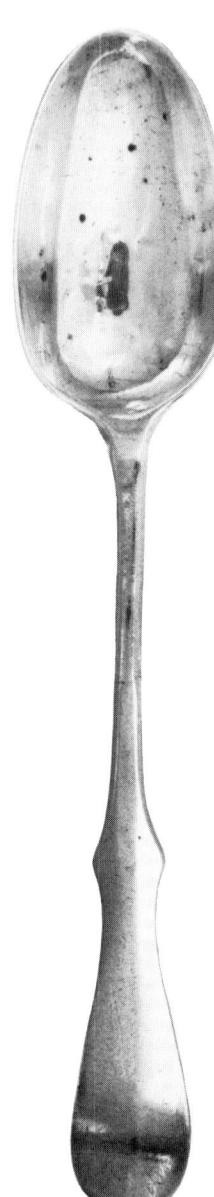

Louis XIV style. While the royal court and wealthy courtiers had their spoons decorated with rich shell motifs, people of lesser means ate with a much simpler spoon, with an oval bowl and rat-tail attachment, similar to the Hanoverian spoon of Britain, with the end turned up. Such spoons existed in France at least from the year 1700 onward.

The eighteenth century gave birth in France to a number of variations in the manner of embellishing spoons. First, it is also around 1700 that the rat-tail attachment of bowl to stem was superseded by the drop and the double drop, which appeared almost simultaneously in Britain, Holland and Germany. Soon the French added another element which was never taken up in Britain. The upper end of the bowl was drawn some way up the stem to form a shouldered stem. This style has remained very popular on the Continent and is still in use today. But the most common French style of the eighteenth century was probably developed from the fiddle pattern spoon. The sides of the fiddle were simply straightened up to form what the French call a spatula, and the rounded top was decorated with a tear drop at the very end. (The type in which the stem merged in a soft curve into the spreading terminal was adopted much later, at the beginning of the nineteenth century and wrongly called the fiddle pattern.) It was either very simple, decorated with the tear drop, or else ornamented, with a shell-shaped relief at the top of the stem terminal.

It was also very early in the eighteenth century that the French adopted the habit of decorating the stem terminals with the owner's initials and coat of arms, a habit which has persisted ever since. Of course other countries followed soon: all through the eighteenth century, everybody in Europe imitated French fashions. The shell pattern was probably the most frequently copied ornamentation.

One of the main French patterns for spoons, and one of the prettiest, emerged during the first half of the eighteenth century, during the Louis XV period, and it was not in the rococo style that one might have expected. This spoon had a flat upturned stem, of the fiddle pattern, decorated with a shell at the upper part of the stem

Table spoon known as the Scots fiddle, in silver, by David Warnock, Glasgow, circa 1750. This type, not known in England, was probably adopted in Scotland from French designs. *National Museum of Antiquities of Scotland*

90

and a clasp at the lower part of the fiddle, the stem edge being further decorated with a double thread. The drop attachment of stem to bowl was shouldered. Such a spoon is typical of the Louis XV style, the clasp for instance being used widely in all decorative arts of the period. But most of the continental spoons were made, not after the Louis XV style, but following what might be called the provincial French styles. These spoons, which can be found in practically all continental countries, are very simple: just a shell at the terminal of the stem, no thread, but with a rib along the centre of the frontal part of the stem. Spoons of the spatulate end style can be found in many countries, including France of course, with a very simple tear drop at the end of the terminal. Some, nicer to look at, had a shell at the end of the terminal and were further decorated with a double thread. Some spoons are even simpler, equipped with an elongated bowl and a shouldered stem of the spatulate end pattern, with a tear drop at the top and thread edges. All these spoons of the eighteenth century continued to be made throughout the nineteenth, and most of the well-known models are still being made today.

When the Old English pattern became popular in Britain, around 1760, the French were producing spoons in the Louis XVI style, and the best-known spoon of the time had a fluted stem entwined with garlands of laurels, with a grotesque mask at the stem joint. In some unusual cases, the stem itself consists of two entwined twigs.

A remarkable fact is that for reasons unknown the French designers never decorated their spoons with well-known rococo motifs, as one would have expected them to do in the eighteenth century, even when the rococo style reached its peak. Apparently they were never tempted. This development was left to south Germany, mainly the great silversmiths of the town of Augsburg, who produced lavish spoons with rococo relief ornaments. The exuberance of these German rococo spoons far outdid the French. Augsburg produced some marvellous, even if rather over-elaborate, rococo breakfast sets which of course included spoons. But it also made simpler flatware in the French styles, which were cheaper alternatives to the Parisian models.

While everybody else was copying the styles created in Paris, the British went their own way. In the seventeenth century they had adopted the trefid-end spoon and probably, but not certainly, the rat-tail attachment, but until the end of the eighteenth century they stayed clear of the general European trend. When Augsburg was producing the most atrocious rococo spoons imaginable, the French, with some restraint one must admit, were making their spoons in the Louis XV and Louis XVI styles, the British remained faithful to much simpler patterns. First came the Hanoverian, and starting around 1770 this was decorated with an engraved ornament following the contours of the stem, the 'feather edge', which in turn was copied on the Continent. Simultaneously with the succeeding English pattern appeared a rather short-lived style, the 'Onslow' type of spoon, with a deeply fluted terminal in the shape of a curled scroll. According to all authors, this pattern never became very popular and only lasted between 1745 and 1775.

The threaded edge was never adopted in eighteenth-century Britain, and the French shouldered stem was practically unknown until about 1770, when some Old English style spoons appeared with the shoulder junction of stem to bowl, and when the feather-edge pattern became fashionable. The shoulder pattern was adopted and seems to have been moderately popular in Victorian times. Again it appears that the eighteenth-century English stem was never as flat as the French examples.

The British did not absorb French influence again until the beginning of the nineteenth century, when the fluted stem became common and the terminal of the spoon stem was shaped like an oblong panel with slightly incurving sides, giving it a near fiddle profile this time. The top of the stem was decorated with a shell and the lower part of the violin outline with two opposed 'palmettes' similar to those found on French objects of the Directoire and Empire style. This was the well-known King's pattern.

At the end of the eighteenth century, many continental spoonmakers made very pointed spoon bowls, a design which can not be considered as an improvement. Such bowl shapes were in use for decades and several countries, including Holland and Russia, were still producing them around the 1860s.

Spoons for particular uses

The eighteenth century saw many styles and patterns come and go.

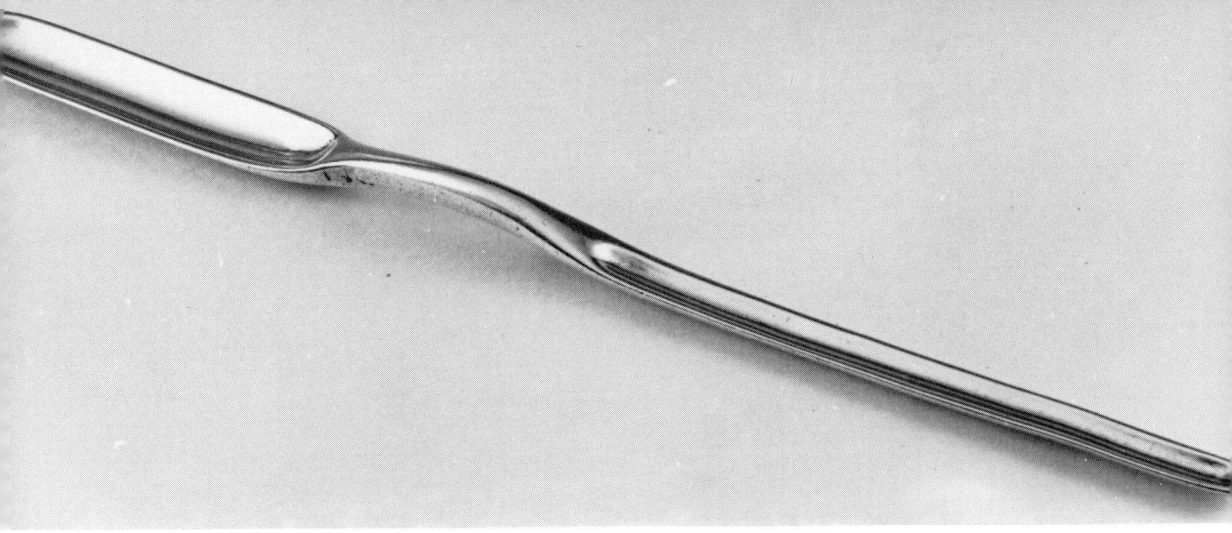

It also saw the advent of the dinner service, with its vast array of spoons of various sizes, table spoons, dessert spoons, coffee spoons and teaspoons, mustard spoons and many others. This was the period when spoons were really made for particular uses, whereas in the previous centuries spoons seem to have been made only to eat solid foods like stews or liquid foods like soups.

One of the most interesting and earliest of all was the controversial *olive spoon*, which began to be made in France, in silver and in pewter, at the end of the seventeenth century. There is however no secret about the olive spoon. With its deep pierced bowl, it was made to take olives out of jars, and nothing is simpler than that. One of the first mentions of such a special spoon is found in the inventory of one Anne de Bellancourt, in France, written in 1720: 'one big soup spoon, two stew spoons, one olive spoon, six coffee spoons, ten table spoons'. Olive spoons figure in many French inventories and wills right from the beginning of the eighteenth century. That the spoons

Dutch silver marrow spoon, hallmark of Den Haarg, 1755. Length 20.7 cm. *Copyright A.C.L., Brussels*

A beautiful caddy spoon made in the form of a leaf, attributed by the Birmingham Assay Office, to Samuel Pemberton, Circa 1800. *Courtesy of the Birmingham Assay Office, Birmingham*

of this name really were used to eat olives is further confirmed by the fact that most of the French eighteenth-century olive spoons were made by the silversmiths of Aix-en-Provence, right in the middle of the olive country. A confusion has been created in Britain by the fact that the mote spoon has sometime been called olive spoon, whereas the olive spoon proper is not equipped with a pointed stem. However, both are equipped with pierced bowls.

The *mote spoon*, so well-known in Britain, is not technically an invention of the eighteenth century, for once spoons themselves had been invented someone was bound to bore holes in the bowl to sift liquids containing impurities or solids. The Brussels Museum has such an antique spoon, in bronze, from the early Middle Ages, pierced roughly with little holes unevenly distributed over the surface of the pear-shaped bowl. In the thirteenth century and probably earlier, Roman Catholic priests used a spoon with a pierced bowl to purify the wine above the chalice before consecration, but of

English silver caddy spoons, all of the leaf pattern, with examples of the 'heart shape' and the 'Roman leaf'. *Courtesy the Worshipful Company of Goldsmiths, London*

course their stems were not spiked, which is a characteristic of the mote spoon.

According to most sources the mote spoon must have appeared somewhere towards the end of the seventeenth century, when they were known as long teaspoons. The spoon is sometimes known as an olive spoon or even mulberry spoon, and while it is unlikely that the British used to eat olives in the eighteenth century, they might have eaten mulberries. And the fruits could be picked up with the spike end of the stem. Mote spoons are in fact a variety of the Roman cochlear, a spoon used to eat shellfish or eggs. They are not found outside Britain, and the Romans and British are the only people to have used spoons equipped with spiked ends. (With one odd exception. The South American Indians noticed that their Spanish conquerors used spoons, previously unknown to them, and they made their own spoons, with a spiked end, sometimes decorated with figures of their own gods, not to eat food with, but to fasten their shawls. Such lovely Indian spoons, in silver or in brass, are hard to find.)

The *coffee spoon* is also mentioned in the inventory of Anne de Bellancourt in 1720, but this type was known in Britain as early as 1703. At the beginning there was probably no difference between the coffee spoon and the teaspoon. When they were first made and used is difficult to say, but it must have been during the second quarter of the seventeenth century. Tea had arrived in England early in the century, and coffee reached Western Europe at about the same time, through the Venetian sailors who traded with Turkey. The very first coffee house was opened in Venice in 1645. Coffee arrived in France a bit later, in the third quarter of the seventeenth century and the French probably thought they needed a small spoon to stir their coffee, while the British and Dutch had the same idea concerning their tea. In most countries coffee and teaspoons date from the late seventeenth century. They were made as a rule exactly like the contemporary table spoons, but of a smaller size. The very first British teaspoons are of the trefid type, plain or engraved with foliate motifs. Another family of teaspoons, created during the eighteenth century, was the spoon with stamped decoration. Spoons with fancy backs were produced in great quantities during the reign of George III. Between 1740 and 1760, some extraordinary teaspoons were produced, encrusted with scrolls or shells, with bowls in the shape of leaves, shells or even acorns. They are decorated back and front. The most numerous examples of eighteenth-century tea-spoons are only decorated with picture backs and are of the Hanoverian or English pattern styles, made during the third quarter of the century. Many copies were produced both later in the eighteenth and in the nineteenth century.

The *mustard spoon*, similar to a miniature ladle, with deep circular bowl of small diameter and a slightly curved stem, appeared first in France and later in Britain. The inventory of a Miss Desmares, from St-Germain, written in 1746, mentions various spoons including *'une cuiller à moutarde'* (a mustard spoon). The inventory was written at the time of the owner's death, and the spoons mentioned were older. Although the document does not give a description of the shape, it may be assumed that there was a marked difference between the mustard spoon and the other spoons that the writer must have noticed. The mustard spoon appeared as such in France around 1725. It was much bigger than today's mustard spoon, for at the beginning people had to mix the dried mustard on their own plate. Mustard spoons as we know them today, made to match a little mustard pot, appeared later, somewhere around 1760.

The *caddy spoon*, like the mote spoon, is hardly ever found outside Britain. It was used to measure tea into the teapot. Apparently it was not made before 1770, people having previously used a kind of ladle to take their tea from the tea caddy. A typical caddy spoon is about 7 to 9 cm long, short-stemmed, with a great variety of bowls. These spoons can be either plain or fanciful in the extreme. For a long time every form of shell or leaf was used, particularly for the bowl itself. It is possible today, providing one lives in Britain, to quickly assemble a sizeable collection of caddy spoons of the eighteenth and nineteenth centuries. Cast examples are rather rare on the market, but include such rare subjects as the famous jockey cap, the eagle's wings, the salmon and the shell type. In the early nineteenth century, the output of caddy spoons became enormous, and the Birmingham 'toymen' let their imagination run riot. Quite a lot of caddy spoons were also made in old Sheffield plate in the late eighteenth and early nineteenth century, particularly the leaf and shell types and of course the jockey cap type. Starting in the 1840s,

Above: Russian silver spoons decorated in niello with Moscow monuments. Coll. de Prins, Brussels.

Below: Russian silver spoons of western design, with shouldered stems (Moscow, 1878). Coll. de Prins, Brussels.

Above, left to right: Russian enamel spoon (Moscow, end of 19th century). Coll. de Prins, Brussels; two tiny Russian silver coffee spoons (Moscow 1874).

Below: Large Russian enamel serving spoon (Moscow 1886—1908). Coll. de Prins, Brussels.

Above: Two Russian silver spoons with shouldered stems (Moscow 1865 and circa 1900).

Below: Russian silver gilt spoons, with bowls decorated in niello with foliage design (Moscow 1860).

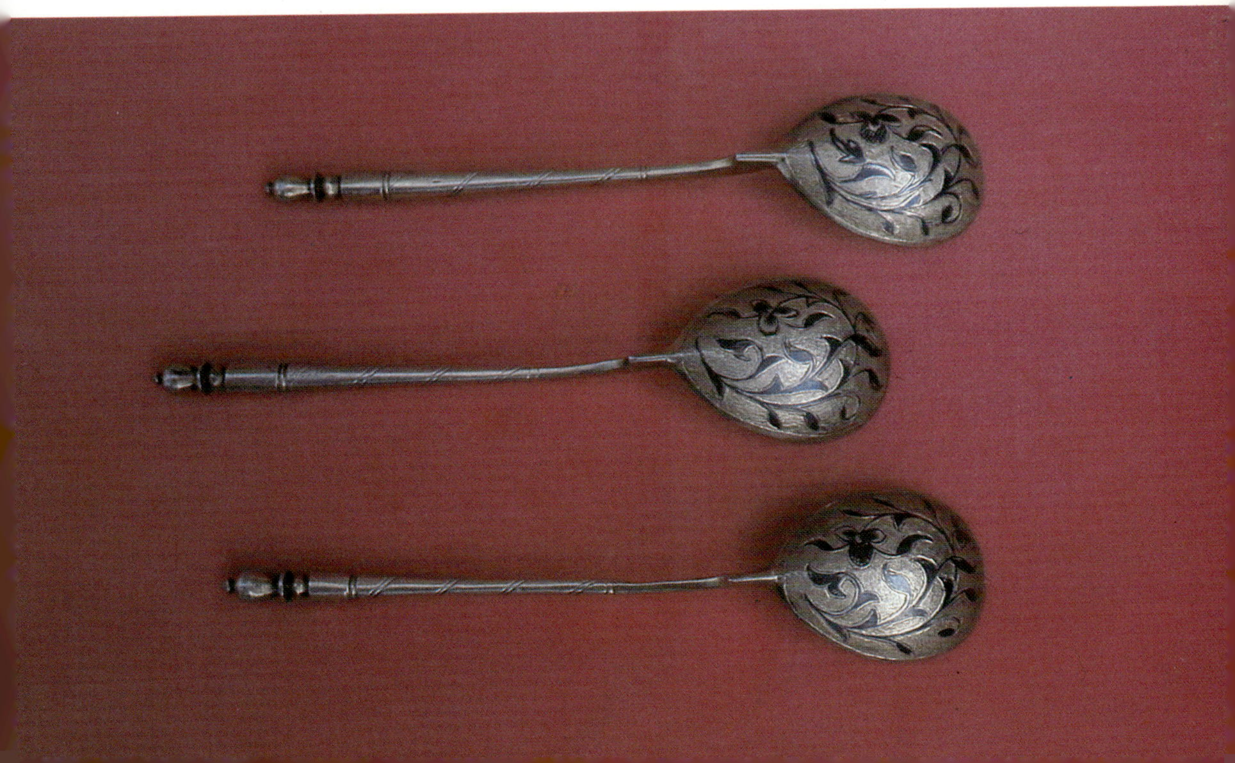

Above: Two Russian silver spoons with bowls engraved with architectural designs (Moscow 1868).

Below: Three English silver spoons. Pictureback tablespoon, decorated with a squirrel surrounded by acorns and oak leaves (George Hindmarsh, London 1764); trefid spoon with egg-shaped bowl and ribbed and reeded rat-tail (Jonathan Bradley, London 1696); Pictureback tablespoon, decorated with crowned double-headed eagle (Richard Palmer?, London 1759). Courtesy Phillips Fine Art Auctioneers.

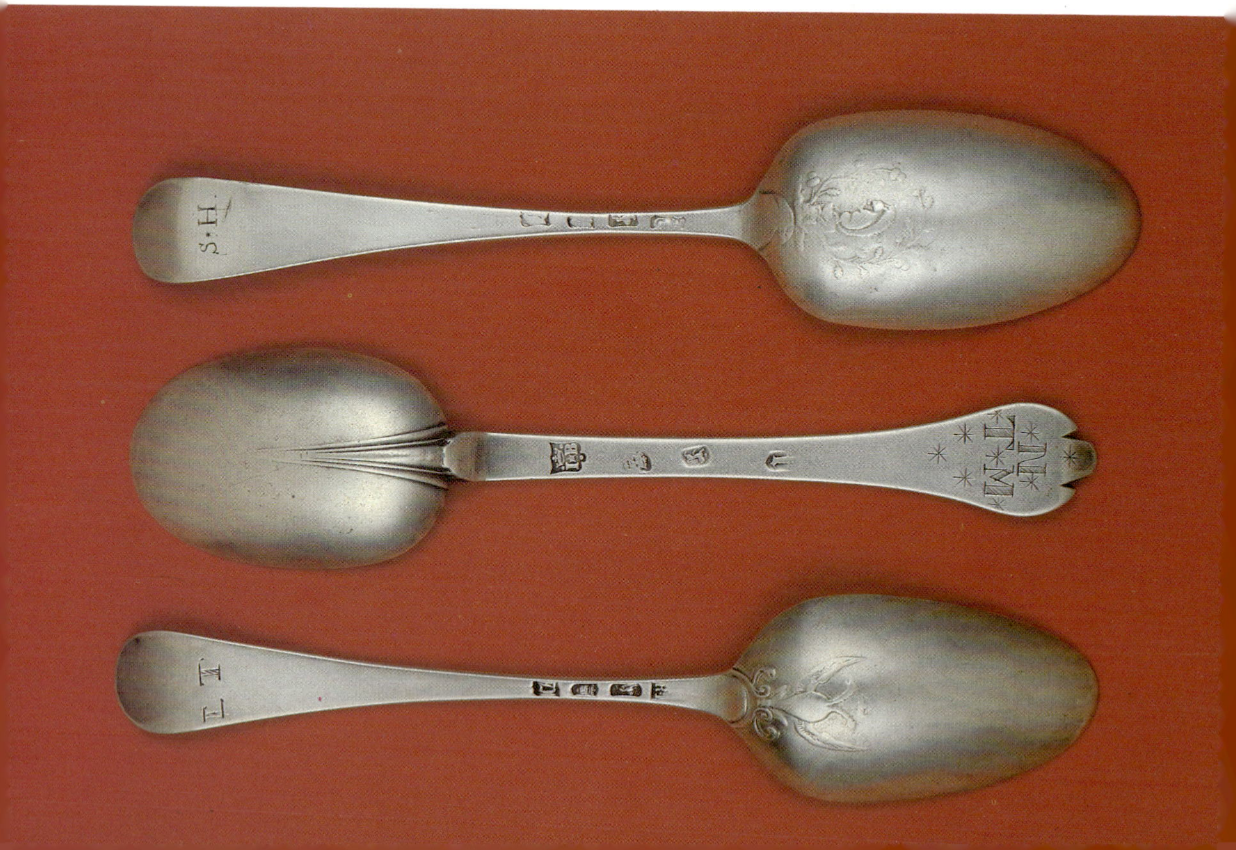

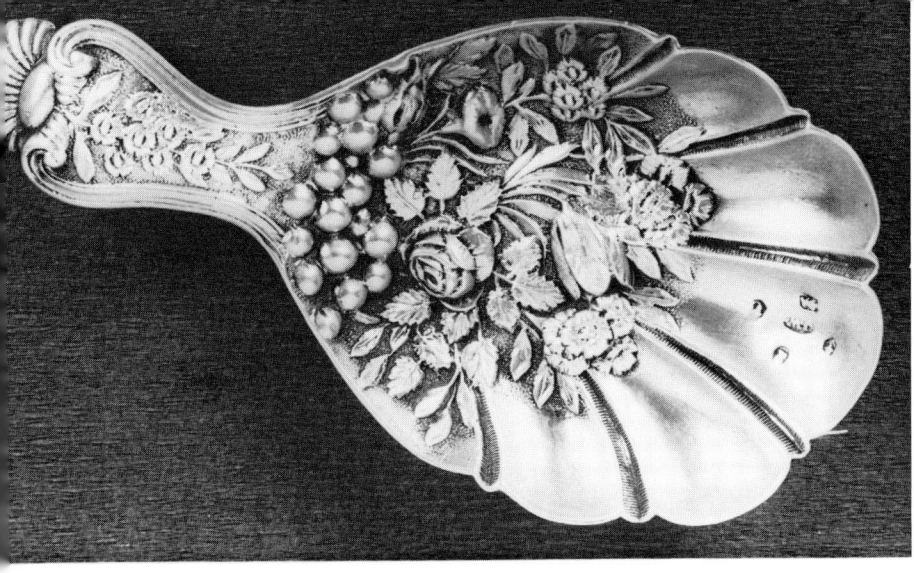

Caddy spoon in silver
gilt by Joseph
Willmore, of
Birmingham, dated
1817; 8 cm long.
*Courtesy of the
Birmingham Assay
Office, Birmingham*

millions of caddy spoons were produced in electroplate.

Another spoon which became individuated during the eighteenth century in Britain and elsewhere was the *dessert spoon*, though there is nothing very particular about its style or shape. It appeared around the middle of the century, when dinner services became common. The small dessert spoons, slightly bigger than but otherwise identical to the teaspoons, are practically always of the style in fashion at the time of their making—possibly Hanoverian or Old English pattern in Britain, Louis XV or Louis XVI in France, or anywhere else in Europe. Since then dessert spoons have been made by the million in silver, silver plate, Sheffield plate, in electroplate, German silver, in fact in any metal.

Feeding spoons were also made during the eighteenth century, but this type of spoon presents the collector with a problem. Whereas we know exactly what a nineteenth-century feeding spoon looked like, we have no idea what they were like in previous centuries. For spoons made for feeding infants or sick persons were made a long time ago. A kind of feeding spoon existed in at least France and Germany as early as the sixteenth century. Some authors call them medicine spoons, and in most French documents they are referred to as *'cuillers d'apothicaires'* (pharmacist's spoons) or *'cuillers de malade'* (sick person's spoons). Some other documentary sources reveal the name *'biberon'* (child's feeding bottle). The extant sixteenth-century models, such as one published by Henri d'Allemagne, have a deep circular bowl and a spout to the bowl at the opposite side of

97

the stem attachment. We have seen that the issue is clouded by some authors' conviction that this odd spoon was mainly used as a sauce boat.

Later examples were probably similar to the papboats for feeding infants, made right from the beginning of the eighteenth century in Britain and on the Continent. These were normally small spoons with an oval body tapering at one end. But feeding spoons have been made in various shapes, an early example being the size of a dessert spoon with a much shorter stem. A well-known type, made throughout the nineteenth century, mainly in Britain and France, is a spoon with a covered bowl and a tubular handle, known in Britain as a 'castor oil spoon'. Feeding spoons, variously called medicine or castor oil spoons, papboats and other names, can be found in silver, silver plate and pewter in most European countries, and some superb examples in silver are of French origin.

A spoon which as a rule is not very much collected is the *salt spoon*. No one seems able to put a date to the birth of the urge to have a special small spoon to pick up salt, but it was not before the beginning of the eighteenth century. For a long time, salt was taken up with the tip of the knife, and the first salt spoons were of the shovel type. Now shovel-type spoons were already made during the Middle Ages. Victor Gay illustrates such a shovel-type spoon in silver gilt, dating from the fifteenth century, the shovel itself looking more or less like the porch of a church, with a saint in relief placed at the top of the shovel. The inside of the shovel is engraved with foliate motifs and its stem is terminated by an acorn in enamel. Was it used to pick up salt? Nobody knows. In any case it can be considered as the ancestor of all the shovel-type salt spoons which started being made at the beginning of the eighteenth century. The shovel-type spoon for picking up salt has survived right up to the present day, but around the mid-eighteenth century circular bowls were made, with a whip-tongue stem, another type which is still produced. Small salt spoons were most likely associated with the

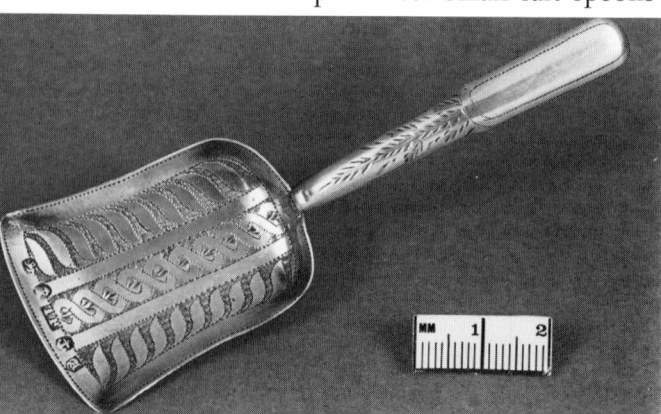

Caddy spoon by Thomas Freeman of Birmingham, dated 1824; 10 cm long. *Courtesy of the Birmingham Assay Office, Birmingham*

introduction around 1760 of the small salt-cellar, which replaced the huge standing salt containers of former times, and were to remain small for ever after.

Another controversial spoon, the *snuff spoon*, made its appearance during the eighteenth century. Very small in size, even those made in silver are generally not hallmarked. They were used from the turn of the century until about 1730 to take snuff out of the very beautiful snuff boxes which were made at the time. Snuff was an awful habit which spread all over Europe during the eighteenth century, but as far as we know, spoons were never sold together with the snuff boxes, and today it is difficult to tell the difference between a snuff spoon and a toy spoon. Toy spoons were made in England and in Holland during the eighteenth century, but tiny as they are they were very often replicas of larger contemporary table spoons, and their style might be the only indication helping to determine the period of their making.

A last type of special spoon appeared during the eighteenth century in various countries of Europe. It was the *marrow spoon*, designed to eat bone marrow, which was once considered as a delicacy. Considering the number of these spoons still in existence, marrow must have been very much appreciated by eighteenth-century gourmets, and silversmiths immediately produced a spoon fit for the job. Two different types were made in all countries. One has a wide channel at one end and a narrow one at the other; another version is double-ended, with a normal spoon bowl at one end and a handle formed as a marrow spoon (or scoop) at the other.

The oldest recorded marrow spoon is from the end of the seventeenth century. Early eighteenth-century marrow spoons often belonged originally to travelling sets. The Augsburg silversmiths for instance never forgot to add at least one such spoon to the breakfast sets they made during the eighteenth century. Spoons of the same type as the British examples were made not only in Germany but also in some numbers in the Low Countries and in France. Marrow spoons were produced in Britain both in greater quantities and for a much longer time than anywhere else. They were made in silver, silver plate, Sheffield plate and also electroplate. It is difficult to collect these spoons on the Continent, but rather easy in Britain.

9 SPOONS FOR SPECIAL OCCASIONS

For reasons impossible to trace, spoons have long been given as presents on very special occasions such as births, deaths, betrothals and weddings. They have been made and sold to commemorate important events in the life of nations, or to celebrate historical events. The ancient guilds, for instance, seem to have been very fond of spoons, mainly in England and in Holland. They were given by people entering the guild and by the guild to people leaving it. Many of these spoons have nothing special about them however, although they are very much sought after by eager collectors. Likewise many commemorative spoons are just simple spoons of the type in fashion at the time of the celebrated occasion, but then they carry inscriptions as to leave nobody in doubt.

Souvenir spoons have been sold all over the world for generations, and they still are. They can be found in every international airport, and in the thousands of souvenir shops that cater for the world tourist trade. These souvenir spoons, or airport spoons, are mostly decorated with the arms of the city where they are sold. As they are cheap souvenirs of a trip abroad, they are very rarely in silver, most of them being in stainless steel. Apart from those spoons decorated with city arms, the traveller will come across souvenir spoons of all types, but always of the teaspoon size. They must carry very fancy finials not always even vaguely related to the visited place or town, and spoons with finials representing the Eiffel Tower can easily be found in Britain.

The variety of finials is tremendous: Big Ben, the Houses of Parliament, the Brussels Atomium, the Acropolis of Athens, the bust of William Shakespeare and many other poets, politicians, musicians and anything else. All the famous monuments are represented on souvenir spoons, all the important persons, even the apostles. For apostle spoons are still being made today, very often in silver. Some beautiful examples are still produced by the firm of Niekerk, in Schoonhoven (Holland), and nothing would be easier than to acquire a complete set of apostles. They are sold today to be used as birth presents or as souvenir spoons. These spoons, so easy to acquire, are collected by some people who enjoy having them, but they are not collectables as far as real spoon collectors are concerned.

Left: A Dutch silver William and Mary spoon, dated 1680, with the inscription in Dutch on the reverse of the spoon: 'Ter eere van Koning & Koningin van St Juns Schut' ('In honour of the King and Queen from St Juns Schut'). *Copyright A.C.L., Brussels; Musee Curtius, Liege*

Right: Back and front views of a dutch 18th century wedding spoon, by G. Minnema of Sneek. The inscriptions on the reverse of the spoon reads '1783. De 29 October is getrout Albert Sijberene and Trintje Rintjes'. *Het Nederlands Openluchtmuseum, Arnhem*

Souvenir spoons can be had by the thousand in a very short time, with perhaps one exception. It has not yet occurred to many spoon collectors that souvenir spoons were also made during the Art Nouveau period, about eighty years ago. These little Art Nouveau spoons, decorated with flowers and insects in the well-known style of the period, can still be picked up. Of course they will not have been made in the town where they were sold, and some might very well carry the word 'Suomi' (for Finland), but be made in France or in Holland. The Art Nouveau spoons of the souvenir type are only sometimes in silver, most of them being in electroplate or in a white metal alloy known as 'alpacca' or 'German silver'.

Souvenir spoons, whether in silver or in any other metal, do not generally interest collectors of antiques, who have a much better field at their disposal. For instance they can and do collect Dutch birth spoons. It seems that apostle spoons were given as presents in England as early as the sixteenth century, but none of the extant examples ever carry a mention to that effect. The giving of spoons as birth presents is corroborated by the writings of Shakespeare and Samuel Pepys, but they never indicate that the spoons they have in mind are of the apostle type. By contrast, the beautiful Dutch birth spoons were engraved with appropriate inscriptions giving the child's name and the date and place of birth. The Dutch started giving spoons to newborn infants at least as early as the seventeenth century, therefore later than in England.

Starting in the sixteenth century, children from the Low Countries (Belgium and Holland) and what is now the North of France, a well-defined corner of Europe, received money—a very sensible idea, even if not very elegant. In the seventeenth century they often received a toy in the shape of a rattle in silver, sometimes in gold, and often decorated with a piece of coral. Such rattles also existed in England in the sixteenth century, but examples are rare before the middle of the eighteenth. Rattles of Belgian or Dutch origin are numerous and can be found in many collections.

The idea of giving a silver spoon for a present at birth survived until the nineteenth century, when people probably thought silver was too expensive as a give-away present. (Although some people in France and Belgium, for instance, went on giving silver beakers as presents as late as the beginning of the Second World War.) The

Dutch birth spoons, examples of which are now in many museums, are not always fancy and are not at all like the apostle spoons. Most of them are quite normal spoons, table spoons of the pied de biche or dognose types, but with suitable inscriptions to mark the occasion. Some recorded ones have all sorts of beautiful finials—saints, apostles, allegorical figures, sailing ships, horses and other ornaments.

The Germans, like the British, the Dutch and some Belgians, also gave spoons to celebrate a birth, but the inscriptions engraved on them are not as clear as the Dutch ones. Also, some of the Dutch spoons found today are not always genuine, as many reproductions have been made since they began to be collected in the later nineteenth century, and one must be careful when acquiring such a spoon. Genuine Dutch birth spoons often appear in England.

Another family occasion which justified the giving of a spoon was a wedding or wedding anniversary. These wedding spoons are similar to the birth spoons, except of course for the inscriptions. They appeared in Holland as early as the sixteenth century, and they are easy to identify because they always carried the appropriate message, such as a statement testifying that Mr So-and-So married Miss So- and-So or Mr and Mrs So-and-So celebrated their wedding anniversary on a given date.

Apart from offering spoons on the occasion of births or weddings and wedding anniversaries, the Dutch also inscribed spoons to mark someone's death, as a *memento mori*. Why a spoon, God only knows. It is rather unusual, but a fact. The Scots and the people of Yorkshire seem to have been the only ones in Britain to adopt this macabre fashion. Their death spoons are of the famous disc finial type, the disc on top of the stem being adorned with a skull. One of these, from the time of Charles II, was sold by a firm of Salisbury auctioneers for the respectable sum of £840 in 1980. It carried a York hallmark, and both sides of the flat stem were engraved with the usual inscriptions 'Live to die' and 'Die to live'.

More cheerful spoons were also made to celebrate or com-

Norwegian wooden wedding spoon. *Norsk Folkemuseum, Oslo*

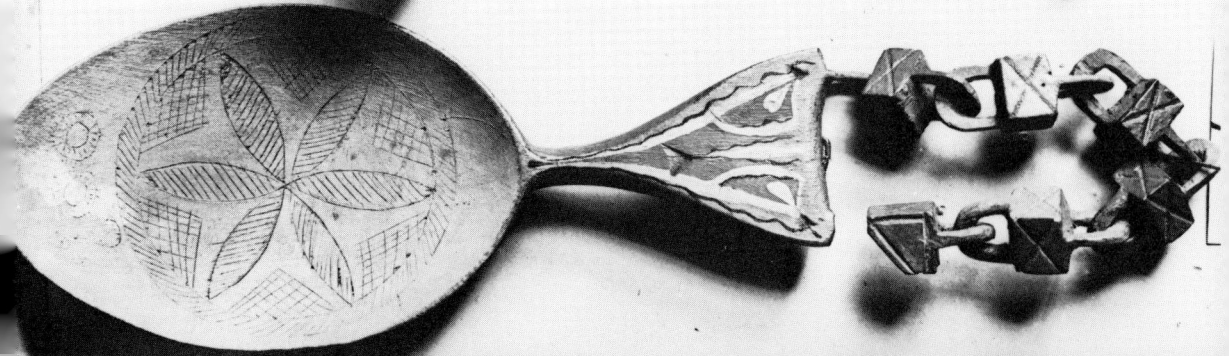

memorate historical events, the most famous examples being the William and Mary spoons made to celebrate the wedding of William of Orange and Mary, daughter of the Duke of York, the future James II. Other similar spoons were produced to celebrate their accession to the British throne. The wedding started a wave of enthusiasm in Holland, more so than in England, and spoons soon started being made, some in silver of course, but mainly in pewter. The main type is rather old-fashioned, even for the end of the seventeenth century. Its finial represents a royal couple, crown on head, sceptre in hand, and arm in arm. The enthusiasm was such that the spoon kept being made long afterwards, and poor-quality pewter ones can still be found in most flea markets for a few francs or pence. Those of Dutch origin always have a circular bowl, for Dutch pewterers went on making this type well into the nineteenth century. Some other William and Mary spoons are of the normal type, such as pied de biche or dognose, engraved with the portraits of the royal couple and sometimes some relevant inscription.

Another well-known and much-admired commemorative spoon is the guild spoon, a type which is found both in England and the Low Countries, usually produced in silver, at least in the seventeenth and eighteenth centuries. After all, the guilds had considerable financial

 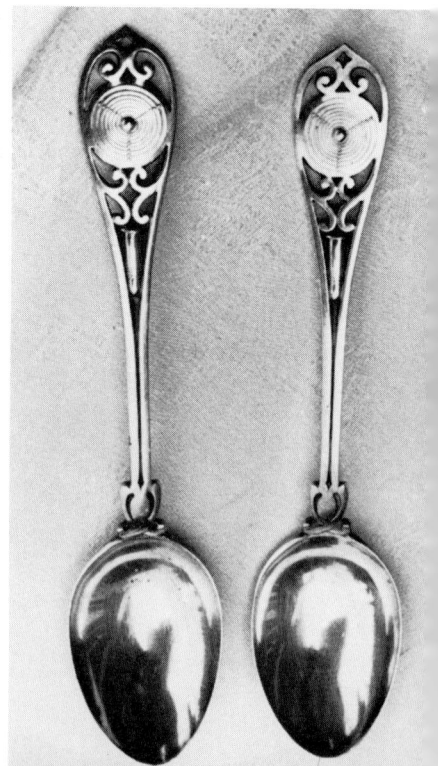

Left: Norwegian wooden wedding spoon. *Norsk Folkemuseum, Oslo*

Right: Two unusual silver English spoons, made in Birmingham in 1904, master's mark W.P. Probably made for a rifle association? *Author's collection*

means, and acquiring silver was no problem to their members. Some of these spoons were also given as prizes in military competitions, for the towns of Belgium and Holland practically all had military guilds, such as fencers, archers, etc. Spoons might be given as rewards for their military achievements and sharp shooting capabilities (but more often they only received a plate in earthenware, hand-decorated with the emblems of the guild).

British livery companies often demanded the entrance fee of a spoon from persons taking the livery. The Court of Armourers and Braziers, for instance, has today a collection of seventy-two antique spoons, because it requested in the sixteenth century that anyone joining the company should present a silver spoon. The same instructions were given by the Exeter Company of Merchant Tailors. The London Innholders Company has twenty-one spoons bearing the figure of St John the Hospitaler, and the London Guildhall Museum has a magnificent collection of six guild spoons dated 1560 which once belonged to the Painters' and Stainiers' Company of London.

Silver guild spoons are mentioned in countless inventories of long ago, and in most European countries. The Dutch guilds too were very keen on the practice. Van der Kellen, a nineteenth-century author, illustrates a pair of spoons belonging to the Musketeers' Guild of Haarlem. These silver spoons, 19·5 cm long, had different finials. One represents a musketeer—an obvious choice for such a group. The other finial is a lion sejeant holding a shield engraved with the arms of the company, two crossed muskets. The beautiful little musketeer of the first spoon holds a musket in his right hand and a shield in the other. Many other guild spoons are illustrated in the delightful book on old silver spoons written by E. M. Klijn, published in 1967, among them one belonging to the Tailors' Guild of Leeuwaarden, with a finial which represents a kneeling monster holding between his two front paws a shield engraved with a pair of scissors, needle and thread. Others come from the Sailors' Guild of Harlingen, a small harbour on the north-west coast of Holland. There is even one belonging to the Broommakers of the town of Hoorn. Hundreds of guild spoons can be found in museums, some of them not fancy at all, but simple table spoons engraved with suitable inscriptions.

One of the most important spoons made for special occasions is the love spoon, found in silver, wood, pewter, and even in brass in some cases. Silver love spoons appeared for the first time in the fifteenth century or even earlier, most of them with finials representing an embracing couple. The Bodo Glaub collection, in Cologne, has such a spoon which probably belongs to the early Middle Ages. It has a short stem of square section and a pear-shaped bowl, which might help to place the spoon as fourteenth- or possibly fifteenth-century. Henri d'Allemagne had a similar spoon in his collection, but in bronze, not silver. It too had a short stem, of the fist spoon type, and was square in section with a pear-shaped bowl. The finial portrays an embracing couple. D'Allemagne attributed his spoon to the thirteenth century, but such an early date is doubtful, and it was probably made during the fifteenth century. Such ancient love spoons are of course extremely rare on the market, and it is only by the greatest of luck that one might see one for sale.

Love spoons were still produced in the following centuries, notably in the Low Countries, but many cheaper ones were made in boxwood in Wales, Norway, the Low Countries, France and Germany. It is not well-known in Britain that the Dutch produced some beautiful wooden love spoons during the sixteenth and seventeenth centuries. These 'bruidlepels' or 'bride spoons' were carved by bridegrooms and given as presents to the loved ones before the wedding. They always carried inscriptions which left no doubt about the carver's feelings.

Van der Kellen illustrated just such an interesting spoon, a real masterpiece, in his *Antiquities of the Low Countries*, without specifying its exact origin, which might have been Holland or Flanders. The stem displays the forms of two lovers with arms round each other's waist. It is connected to the oval bowl by the figure of a woman who holds the bowl between her legs. The inscription on the reverse of the bowl reads:

My everlasting love
Accept what I am sending you
Although it is rather futile
God knows it comes from the heart.

As if it was not enough, another inscription is carved inside the bowl:

> My love, keep your love like a tree keeps its branches and don't let it go until you die.
> My heart I share with you
> If you break it
> God will avenge me.

Norwegian wooden wedding spoon. *Norsk Folkemuseum, Oslo*

One of the best-known kinds of love spoon is the Welsh, although many people are not aware that similar spoons were made in France, Norway and Germany. The Welsh love spoons, carved in quite a variety of woods—sycamore, beech, oak, pine, box, yew, fruit woods, etc.—seem to have been made from the seventeenth until well into the nineteenth century. Some are still being made today, but mostly for the tourist trade. They were carved by young men in love, young men from little villages lost in the Welsh valleys, who painstakingly carved spoons out of a single block of wood, often with a simple knife. They were given as engagement presents, and then displayed for many years above the hearth, once they had been accepted by the courted lady.

Usually two spoons, parallel to each other, were carved from a block and decorated with chip-carving, producing a shallow faceted ornamentation. The flat panel to which the two spoons were attached was often decorated with a great variety of pierced motifs, such as hearts, keys, keyholes, wheels, crowns, stars, anchors and many other designs. Most of these motifs were in fact symbols. The wheels meant: 'I'll work for you', and the keyholes: 'My house is yours.'

The Scandinavians, mainly the Norwegians, who more than others lived in remote villages and had nothing much to do in the winter anyway, also used love spoons to show their love. The young man carved his spoon and gave it to the girl of his choice as an invitation to accept him as a suitor. By accepting such a gift, the girl of course committed herself. The Norwegian spoons, some of which go back to the eighteenth century, are normally of two types. One is a spoon attached to a flexible chain carved out of a single piece of wood. The other model consists of two spoons joined together by a flexible chain. That Welsh and Norwegian young men should carve love spoons out of wood seems to be a normal enough spare time

107

occupation. What the Africans were doing with their spoons, and why they carved them out of wood in the Norwegian manner, chain and all, is more mysterious. For it appears that the Norwegian type of spoon was made in Central Africa, and one example is in the Bodo Glaug collection, in Cologne. Wedding spoons were also produced in France, but apparently Gallic lovers were not as keen as in Wales or Norway: instead of carving their own spoons, they just bought them in markets or fairs. The Spaniards too had love spoons, with large bowls and stems formed as the figure of a man and a woman in profile.

Another spoon for special occasions which has not yet been mentioned is the rifle competition spoon, one of which is illustrated in this book. This rather charming model was made by a Blackburn silversmith, William Priestland, at the turn of the century. (Hallmark: W.P.). Until the beginning of the Second World War, according to Mr S. E. F. Beechey, Assay Master of the Birmingham Assay Office, who identified the not very well known Blackburn silversmith, there were many rifle clubs in Britain, some from firms (like the Birmingham Assay Office Rifle Club), others from public houses. Competitions were on a 'home' and 'away' basis, with leagues as with football and internal competitions for club members were also held, on a handicap basis. In some cases sets of spoons were given as prizes. The Blackburn example has its stem decorated with a target above a bullet.

One special occasion is Christmas, and nobody except the Danes has ever thought of giving spoons as Christmas presents. The fashion seems to have started rather late, around the turn of the century, when Danish craftsmen began producing Christmas spoons, mostly in silver, decorated with brilliant enamels. The spoons produced just before the First World War are not of the Art Nouveau style as one might expect. Their stems were more prosaically decorated with all kinds of Christmas designs, such as angels, mistletoe, the star of Bethlehem, Copenhagen cathedral, the Virgin Mary, the infant Christ, the three Wise Men, kneeling shepherds, and Father Christmas and his reindeer. These Danish silver spoons, all of teaspoon size, and very bright, are the only commemorative spoons which could be collected today without undue difficulty.

10   THE RUSSIAN SPOONS

For centuries the Russians, probably more than anybody else in the whole wide world, have produced some of the most beautiful spoons one could hope to possess. Today's collectors, wherever they are, can choose from a very wide selection, since Russian spoons, made in silver, enamelled or nielloed, before the October Revolution which marks the end of the Tsarist empire, are not at all rare, strange as it seems. It is as if thousands of the Russian refugees who fled the Revolution had made saving their spoons their first priority. The great quantity of Russian spoons now on the market does not keep the dealers' prices down, yet it must be admitted that most of the Russian spoons of the pre-communist era are a delight to look at, and silver spoons from other countries can hardly stand the comparison. Russian spoons of various types offer collectors the chance to build up a quite sensational collection in a rather short time, providing of course they have the necessary financial means. But how on earth did all those magnificent spoons get out of Russia?

Of course, there seem to have been tremendous numbers of decorative spoons made in Russia during the nineteenth century. They were produced in all the silver towns, from northern Archangel, on the White Sea, to southern Odessa, on the Black Sea, the highest percentage being made and hallmarked in the two main silver centres of St Petersburg and Moscow. The spoons which accompanied the exodus of people fleeing the Bolsheviks were either antiques or might have been bought only a few years earlier in the workshops of Moscow, Vologda, Veliki Ustyug and other towns. Sometimes they were still in their original boxes. They were sold for peanuts during the roaring Twenties, because not only Russian spoons but Russian silver in general simply did not interest many people in western Europe for a very long time.

For many years Russian silver was practically unknown in

western art circles and only an enlightened few knew of its long history and its richness. One has to remember that even the famous Carl Fabergé did not attract much attention from the art critics when he exhibited in the 1900 Paris Exhibition. It is only very lately, during the last ten years or so, that silver collectors have at last taken notice, causing prices to go higher and higher. Fortunately, spoons being smallish objects, they can still be found at reasonable prices, and are still within reach of the average collector, who has a choice between a few eighteenth-century examples and a host of nineteenth-century ones.

It would be sheer luck to find a Russian spoon of the seventeenth century, and that is rather a pity, for it is the most essential period of development of Russian silver work and artistic skill. Most of the seventeenth-century silverware was made in Moscow, which was then the centre of Russian silver production, a position it retained until the first few years of the eighteenth century, when St Petersburg (now Leningrad) was founded. Beautiful spoons were made in Russia during the seventeenth century, the golden age of Russian silversmithing, including some very plain spoons, with rat-tail attachment. But the real masterpieces were made in cloisonné or painted enamels on silver, with ornaments of leaves, flowers, birds, animals and fishes. Others just as beautiful were produced in nielloed silver, a genre which had been practised mainly in the Byzantine empire, but which was to remain a kind of Russian speciality until the October Revolution. Some nielloed spoons were decorated with the usual emblems on the outside of the bowls: fish, flowers, birds. Some, more mysterious, were decorated with nielloed inscriptions in Slavonic lettering—names, proverbs, good wishes— very difficult to decipher.

All these beautiful Russian spoons of the seventeenth century, including some plain silver ones simply engraved with emblems or inscriptions, can be found today, in all sizes, not in Western antique shops but in Russian museums, such as the Hermitage, in Leningrad, which has a tremendous collection.

The antique spoons cannot be found in western Europe, but fortunately vast quantities of antique Russian spoons were reproduced during the second half of the nineteenth century, enamelled in the old Russian style, in niello or in plain solid silver decorated with inscriptions in Slavonic lettering, the latter looking in fact much older than they are in reality. It is these late Russian examples which can be found today in London, Paris, Berlin, Dublin and Istanbul, together with some pleasant but uninteresting examples of normal flatware, mostly copies from the old French styles. The only difference is that they are stamped with Russian hallmarks. As has been mentioned before, everybody in Europe but the British adopted the French spoon patterns in the eighteenth century, and in the nineteenth too. The Russians were no exception. Single specimens of these very ordinary flatware spoons, which can be found with a rat-tail attachment or a violin-shaped end, are usually sold very cheap, as most collectors are only interested in complete sets. Some Russian flatware was also made in very poor-quality silver, marked with the figure '72' in a shield.

If the Russian flatware is nothing to boast about, it is not due to any lack of imagination in the Russian silversmiths. Peter the Great and the Westernized noblemen of the Russian empire are much to blame. The founder of St Petersburg, new capital of the empire, was determined to Westernize Russia, and his new town must follow the Western fashions even in silversmithing. Peter the Great forced many silversmiths out of Moscow and other silver towns and ordered them to move to St Petersburg, where they met craftsmen from Finland, Sweden, Germany and France. And whether they liked it or not, the goldsmiths and silversmiths had to follow the Western styles.

The Louis XV ornamentation predominated well into the 1760s, when the Russian silversmiths and their Russian-based foreign colleagues departed from the rococo style and its rounded lines and followed everybody else on the Continent in adopting the simple cut shapes and more austere lines of the neo-classical styles. The Russian flatware was now decorated with garlands, wreaths and medallions to match the newly-built houses of St Petersburg. The first quarter of the nineteenth century can be considered as a further development of the neo-classical style, with new motifs of the French Empire style and ornamentation of lion heads, eagles, swans and griffons.

To sum up, the eighteenth-century flatware follows the Louis XV and Louis XVI styles, with the French Empire style predominant during the early nineteenth century. But it would be wrong to

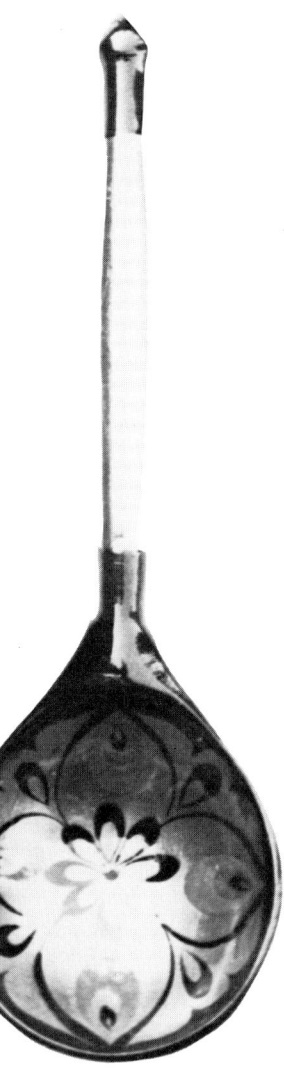

Russian spoon in painted wood, made in Fedoskino, near Moscow.

believe that Russian silversmiths of the eighteenth century only produced Western-looking flatware. For while the St Petersburg craftsmen and their foreign colleagues kept on copying the Western styles, silversmiths in other towns, including Moscow, kept following their traditional styles of the seventeenth century, producing spoons with round bowls, in silver gilt decorated with niello and enamels. Many magnificent spoons of typical Russian style were produced during the eighteenth century in such centres as Moscow, in Tobolsk, the great Siberian silver town, Vologda and Veliki Ustyug. But typical eighteenth-century Russian spoons rarely appear in Western capitals today.

The Russian enamel spoons

If niello has always been a great speciality of the Russian silversmiths, from the Middle Ages until today, it is also safe to state that they have used enamels as a decorating substance more than anyone else. Even today, Western visitors to the numerous 'Berioschkas', the Russian shops which are only open to tourists, can still be convinced that some beautiful modern enamelled articles are still being made in Soviet Russia.

As it is practically impossible to lay hands on seventeenth- or eighteenth-century enamel spoons, most collectors are only concerned with the spoons produced from the middle of the nineteenth century, when a revival promoted by some important silversmiths in Moscow led to the production of millions of spoons too delicate to be of any domestic use, and decorated in the brightest of enamels in the antique manner of the seventeenth century.

And the Russians certainly knew about enamels. The silversmiths of Kievan Russia in the eleventh and twelfth centuries were well acquainted with the cloisonné technique they had inherited from Byzantium. But unfortunately hardly any pieces from Kievan Russia have survived, and few enamel pieces were produced during the following centuries, under the Mongol occupation. It was only at the very end of the fifteenth century, when Moscow had emerged, that the Russians started to use enamels again. And the old cloisonné technique was taken up again in Moscow around the middle of the sixteenth century, mainly in the famous Kremlin workshops, where

112

the favourite colours were white, green and blue of various shades. All objects, including spoons, were decorated with filigree foliage, the flowers being in enamels. It was the beginning of what is now called the 'Old Russian' style, which was purely Russian, at last.

The following century was in fact the golden age of Russian enamelling, and Veliki Ustyug became a great centre for the production of enamels in the cloisonné technique, using a different palette of green, black, yellow and sky-blue on a white background. At the same time another town, Solvychegodsk, in the Urals, produced another type of enamelling. They did not use the cloisonné technique, because the local silversmiths had discovered the technique of painted enamels. And instead of articles of a religious type, they produced domestic wares, making bowls, plates, knife handles and magnificent spoons. All objects were completely covered, inside and outside, with white enamel which they painted with flowers, often tulips, animals such as griffons, and swans, most of the time contained in medallions. This new type of enamelling is known today as 'Usol enamel', distinguishable by an elaborate pattern of flowers. The new technique was very successful in Russia, and silversmiths in other towns, such as Yaroslav, followed suit, also producing many delicate and bright-coloured spoons. Rostov followed the others, and kept going until well into the nineteenth century. But enamels were more or less neglected in Russia from the end of the eighteenth until about the middle of the nineteenth century, when the revival occurred.

The pan-Slavic movement

Everywhere in Russia, but especially in Moscow, starting in the reign of Tsar Nicholas I (1825–55) certain artists and craftsmen began to revive the art and folklore of ancient Holy Russia. The movement spread rapidly, and as it did so the old Russian styles were revived. One well-known Moscow silversmith, Pavel Ovchinnikov, was probably the first to re-create the old technique of cloisonné enamels, which was to meet with great success until the October Revolution. All over the country, in practically all the silver towns, spoons, glorious enamelled spoons, were made by the cloisonné technique. Thousands were produced of all sizes and of all shapes, from tiny coffee and salt spoons to very large serving spoons. Some of these spoons were sold in boxes of six, twelve, eighteen or even twenty-four. They were all made at the time for the home market, as Westerners had little appreciation of the wild magnificence of the Old Russian style.

The spoons made in Russia between the middle of the nineteenth century and the 1917 Revolution are marked by strong contrasting colours, beloved of Russian silversmiths and of course of the Russian people. They all used extra-bright colours, and their palette was very wide indeed, but blue was practically always predominant, notably a piercing sky-blue. One can get a good idea of these spoons by looking at the colour section.

One could carry on indefinitely with such descriptions, as each Russian enameller had his own ideas about the use of colours, and the silversmiths all had their own ideas about spoon design. Although the vast majority of Russian enamel spoons are made using the cloisonné technique, some artists, such as Ovchinnikov himself, used the plique à jour technique around 1900. It should be pointed out here that the Norwegians in Oslo and Bergen were producing very fine spoons using the same technique at about the same time (see Chapter 12).

In most cases, the Russian enamel spoons have the reverse of the bowl decorated with scroll foliage of an immense variety of colours, generally on a matt background, or with the traditional Old Russian geometric designs. Some stems are straight and in plain white silver or silver gilt, sometimes decorated with enamels. Some stems are twisted. The bowls are of various shapes. Some rare caviar spoons have bowls made of birchwood; only the handles are in silver gilt decorated with cloisonné enamels.

The Russian enamel spoons are among the most gorgeous that can be collected today, but unfortunately they are not cheap any more. Collectors, before buying Russian enamel spoons, should always have a very close look at the enamels, as some of these spoons have been knocked about, some parts of the original enamel have cracked, and some cells are just empty.

The Russian nielloed spoons

Russia is the only country in the world where the difficult technique of nielloed silver has been in continuous use for a thousand years. It is a historical fact that the Russian silversmiths knew the technique as early as the tenth century, and the most impressive collection of nielloed objects can be seen today in the Kremlin Museum in Moscow. Niello is a mixture of various ingredients such as silver, copper or pewter, lead and sulphur, but each silversmith always had his own recipe. The ingredients are reduced to powder, then mixed with borax to make a kind of black or grey enamel, depending on the recipe used. The niello technique is a difficult one, for it takes patience and a very sure hand to draw the design on the silver, and then to chase it with the greatest of care so that the deep grooves can be filled with the niello. The article in question then has to be put in an oven, where it remains until the niello becomes as hard as metal. The well-known solidity of niello explains why so many antique items have managed to survive and are still extant. After removal from the oven, the article has to be cleaned and polished.

The technique of niello flourished in Russia during the sixteenth and seventeenth centuries, but most of the pieces from that period were never marked. Magnificent pieces were made, and included beakers, mugs, tankards, plates, flasks, patens and spoons, entirely covered with motifs in niello such as flowers, birds, fruits and beasts. The seventeenth-century spoons in nielloed silver have pear-shaped bowls and stems either of round section or twisted; the finials are often of the well-known seal-top type, or of the acorn type, with a few much more fancy. The Hermitage Museum, one of the greatest in the world, has many seventeenth-century nielloed spoons in its collections. One of the nicest specimens has a stem surmounted by the double-headed eagle of the Romanovs; the inside of the bowl is engraved with a fish, and the bust of a cherub appears midway up the stem. Some of these spoons are decorated with motifs of oriental origin, for instance pomegranates or cypresses, or with motifs inspired by the Ukraine, such as cut flowers.

During the eighteenth century Moscow was the most important centre of production, and its nielloed silver reflected images from classical times, with ornaments such as Greek and Roman soldiers, or else various events taken from mythology, which seem a bit dull next to those objects in niello decorated with scenes taken from Russian everyday life and from the history of Holy Russia. Moscow

Reverse of the bowl of a Russian silver tea spoon, engraved with architectural design. *Author's collection*

was not the only place of production in the eighteenth century, and many northern towns such as Veliki Ustyug, Vologda and Viatka produced magnificent examples. Towards the end of the century, the factories of Veliki Ustyug for instance produced spoons decorated with typically eighteenth-century engravings—flirting young couples and other pastoral scenes. At the very end of the century spoons bowls were decorated with views of monuments in various cities sometimes difficult to identify now.

Tobolsk, in Siberia, also became a well-known niello centre, and many of its spoons were decorated with local views. Spoons were also produced in Irkutsk, Tomsk and Yakutsk. The town of Viatka produced spoons decorated in very black niello with pictures taken from engravings and popular prints. The production of niello spoons must have been tremendous at the beginning of the nineteenth century, for almost every silver town produced them, as is indicated today by the numerous hallmarks found on spoons sold on the Western market.

Niello production was actually intensified during the second quarter of the nineteenth century practically everywhere in Russia, including St Petersburg. Millions of spoons were made for the domestic market, but few were exported commercially. Many are decorated with views of various towns (the Kremlin is one of the favourite subjects), churches, monuments, scenes taken from Russian fairy-tales, figures of peasants working or enjoying themselves, architectural designs. Some, as beautiful as the others, were more simply decorated with foliage designs on bowls and stems. Like the enamel spoons of the Old Russian style, they were sold singly or in boxes. The Russians never stopped using the technique of niello, and spoons of this type are still manufactured in the USSR in Moscow and in Veliki Ustyug, where a 'Northern Niello Factory' still exists.

Russian nielloed spoons are quite easy to find in western Europe, but of course their prices have gone up during the last few years, as there is now a definite interest in Russian silver of the Tsarist period in practically all Western countries.

The Russian hallmarks

If a collector intends to acquire Russian spoons he should get acquainted beforehand with the Russian hallmark system. He must know for instance that it would be pointless to look for a mark on any piece of silverware made prior to the mid-seventeenth century, for the first regulations attempting to inject some order into the ancient craft of silversmithing in Holy Russia dates from the very beginning of the century. The oldest mark discovered on a piece of Russian silver dates from the middle of the seventeenth century, when Moscow silversmiths stamped a double-headed eagle, the eagle of the Romanov coat of arms, on their wares. This mark was to remain in use until the year 1741, but when St Petersburg was founded in 1703 the silversmiths of the new capital adopted the same symbol, and also kept using it until 1741. The well-known double-headed eagle of Moscow was inscribed in various shields, a triangle, a circle or an oval, then in a circle again, the year of manufacture being sometimes added to the eagle. Most of the time, a date-letter in Cyrillic lettering was also inscribed inside the shield, with the year given according to an old chronology supposed to have started at the beginning of the world.

But collectors should beware of double-headed eagles, because other towns besides Moscow and St Petersburg used the same symbol during the eighteenth century—towns such as Veliki Ustyug (1768–82), Galich and Kamenetz-Podolsk at the end of the century, Kaluga (1772–86), Tula at the very end of the century. And the eagle was used right up to the 1917 Revolution on silverware produced by court jewellers like Carl Fabergé, Ivan Morosov, Carl Boianovski, Ivan Sazikov, Ivan Khlebnikov, Pavel Ovchinnikov, Ivan Gubkin, etc.

It was under the reign of Peter the Great that hallmarking became compulsory in the Russian empire when he published a ukase on 13 February 1700. Silversmiths, and therefore spoonmakers, had to stamp their touch mark, consisting of their initials: the initial of the Christian name first followed by the initial of their surname. (Of course, all the initials found on Russian silver are written in Cyrillic lettering, so it is advisable before collecting to learn the Russian alphabet or to have handy a list giving the transliteration of all Russian letters into Roman letters.)

The above summary is given for information only, since most of the

Russian spoons a Western collector can hope to find are of a much later period. In Moscow the Romanov eagle ceased to be used as a town mark in 1741, when the figure of St George in a shield was officially adopted, with the year numerals inside the shield, under the saint. St George was used until the end of the nineteenth century, and many spoons carry this hallmark, the year numerals appearing and disappearing in a most baffling manner. This does not matter, since starting in 1741 the assayer's mark consisting of his two initials above the year numerals inside a rectangle began to be used. In St Petersburg the eagle was replaced, also in 1741, by a hallmark representing a sceptre and two crossed anchors, which remained in use until the end of the nineteenth century. At the same time, all silversmiths working outside Moscow and St Petersburg stamped their own town mark on their silverware.

Starting from the beginning of the eighteenth century, all Russian silverware was stamped with four different hallmarks, as follows:

the town mark;
the master's mark;
the assayer's mark and year numerals;
the standard mark.

A set of six Russian tea spoons in silver gilt. The spoons, made in Moscow in 1860, are decorated with foliage designs in niello. They are still in their original box. *Author's collection*

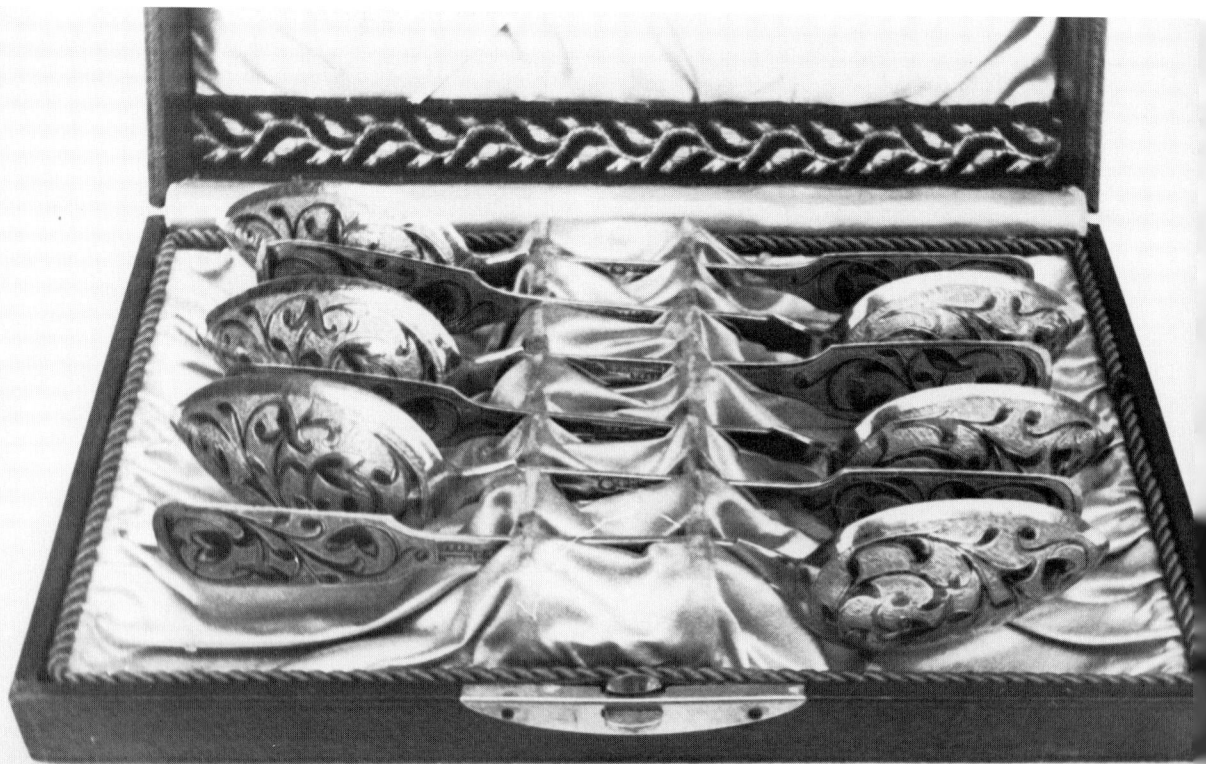

The standard mark gives the number of 'solothniks' in two figures, at first separated from each other, then reunited in one single shield in the third quarter of the eighteenth century.

Let us note straight away that the Russian standard marks differ completely from the marks used in western Europe. The Russian silver standard is based on a quite ancient measuring unit called the solothnik, from the word soloto, meaning gold. One solothnik represents 1/96th of the Russian pound, which is equivalent to 409,5174 g. Pure silver is therefore 96 solothniks. But of course silversmiths do not use pure silver, and most of the Russian spoons bear marks such as 84, 88 or 91, the most common standard being 84, equivalent to 875/1000ths, and the standard 91 is above the sterling standard, equivalent to about 947/1000ths of pure silver.

The four above-mentioned hallmarks were used until 1880, and many many spoons found on today's market belong to that period. Between 1880 and 1890, according to Russian historians, the town mark and the standard mark were enclosed in the same shield.

The kokoshnik era

According to some Western historians a new mark, the famous 'kokoshnik' was adopted for the whole of Russia in 1896, some even say 1899. Both dates remain to be proved, for many pieces examined are marked clearly with the Moscow town mark and the kokoshnik and dated 1890. If the kokoshnik did not appear before 1896, why are pieces marked with it when they are dated 1890? It seems therefore that the kokoshnik, the hallmark of a woman's head turned to the left and wearing the famous Russian headdress of that name, was created in 1890. Half the spoons in circulation today bear this hallmark. Starting in the year 1908, the profile of the woman was turned to the right and so it remained until the October Revolution. In both cases, one can find the kokoshnik alone in a circle, or in an oval together with the standard numerals.

But there is more to it than that. In the shield of the first type of kokoshnik, whether circle or oval, can be seen two very tiny letters in Cyrillic lettering, often illegible. They are the initials of the district assayer, for when the kokoshnik was adopted the whole empire was divided into districts, each one having its own assayers. The second kokoshnik created in 1908 no longer carries the assayer's initials but instead had a single Greek letter which is the clue to the district of manufacture. The Greek letter delta points to the Moscow district, the letter alpha to St Petersburg, kappa to Odessa and so on. The kokoshnik of the first type (profile to the left) does not enable anyone to determine the place or origin, unless they are able to read the initials and know where that particular assayer worked. The 1908 kokoshnik does not give a clue to the assayer's name, but it clearly indicates the district of origin.

Another hallmark which sometimes appears on Russian spoons, not as an additional mark but replacing the usual master's mark, is the artel mark. The artel was a cooperative society of jewellers, silversmiths and goldsmiths working independently. Mostly they sold their wares to the big firms, which sometimes had the cheek to add their own mark to the articles. Beginning in the late nineteenth century, there were many artels in Russia, at least twenty of them, each one with a number, and their silverware was marked with the number in a square. The 6th Artel, working in Moscow, would mark with the number 6 followed by the letters Ya.A in Cyrillic lettering.

Knowledgeable collectors should know that Russian silverware was also exported in the usual manner, long before the Revolution, mainly to the Austro-Hungarian empire, to Poland, and to the three Baltic states which are now part of the Soviet Union. Most of the silver exported to the Austro-Hungarian empire was stamped with the official import mark of the empire, usually in the town of Lvov (formerly Lemberg), the district closest to the Russian border. The hallmark used most was the one added between April 1872 and May 1922, the head of a woman turned to the right, inside shields corresponding to the standard of silver. The shield contained a letter indicating the district of assay. (F for the Ukrainian town of Lvov.)

Foreign hallmarks are liable to appear on pieces of antique Russian silver, as these articles have moved from place to place for many years. One might say that collecting Russian silver, spoons or anything else, is rather full of surprises when it comes to hallmarks, and you cannot expect to be able to identify all the marks found without a wide knowledge of hallmarking in various countries. But as collectors know, identifying hallmarks is all part of the game.

11 SPOONS OF THE NINETEENTH CENTURY

It takes considerable financial means today to be able to collect the magnificent luxury spoons of the Renaissance, either in silver gilt, in silver, or more simply in carved ivory. Some apostle spoons from the sixteenth century reach astronomical prices: one from the time of Henry VIII was recently sold for the sum of £4000, which puts it automatically beyond the reach of the average collector. Of course people could collect contemporary spoons made in less noble metals, like pewter for instance, but most antique pewter spoons are unmarked, and it is tricky to attribute a definite date to them. Very antique spoons of quality are reserved for a few lucky ones, but the modest collector who is keen but not rich could very happily discover what he is looking for in the nineteenth century.

Millions, no, billions, of spoons were made all over the world during the nineteenth century, in all kinds of metals from gold to white alloys, but unfortunately most of them warrant little attention. All the spoons which had been created during the eighteenth century, and sometimes before, were faithfully reproduced during the nineteenth century, and these reproductions offer no scope for collecting. Who wants, for instance, a Louis XV-style silver spoon made in 1900? Not a real collector. And the situation is the same in all countries, even in Britain, where spoons in the Old English pattern are still being produced today. This style was even taken up on the Continent, as it was simple and unpretentious.

Spoons with tapering stems terminated by a teardrop, with or without rib, have been made continually since the eighteenth century. Spoons with tapering round-ended stems with a simple shell on top have never stopped being made, also since the eighteenth century. Spoons with stems terminating in an oblong, with a teardrop at the very end, and with threaded edges, existed in France as early as 1740, and were still in production at the beginning

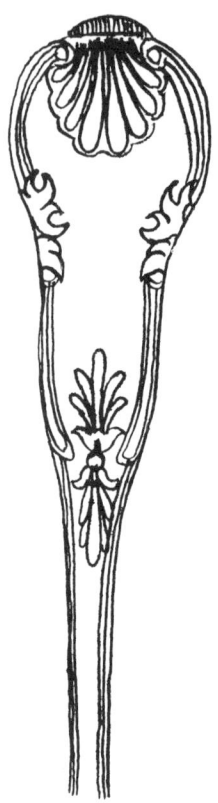

King's pattern.

of the twentieth century. And none of those spoons could be collected, because they are reproductions of earlier styles.

In Britain the situation is somewhat different. The eighteenth-century spoonmakers never adopted any of the French styles, as so many others did in practically all European countries, so their nineteenth-century successors were not tempted into reproducing the French eighteenth-century spoons. But they let themselves be influenced by those French styles. At the beginning of the nineteenth century, we have noted that they produced the now familiar King's pattern, mixing a (timid) violin shape, the shell end and the Directoire 'palmettes' to produce a French-derived spoon which can be found today in silver, in silver plate and even in electroplate. The King's pattern was soon followed by a variety of other patterns, such as the King's husk, which retained the general shape of the King's pattern but with the shell at the top of the stem replaced by a husk. The hourglass pattern was a copy of a well-known Louis XV style. The Queen's pattern and the King's honeysuckle pattern were derived up to a certain point from the old French spoons of the eighteenth century. Many spoons were made in the fiddle thread and shell pattern, fiddle and thread teardrop, fiddle and shell patterns, all French-inspired, and with this special characteristic, that they never had the fiddle shape.

Other more indigenous patterns emerged during Victorian times, and they offer better scope for collecting. These Victorian spoons, in

Front and back views of an English silver spoon of the hourglass pattern, dating from the beginning of the 19th century. *Courtesy of the Worshipful Company of Goldsmiths, London*

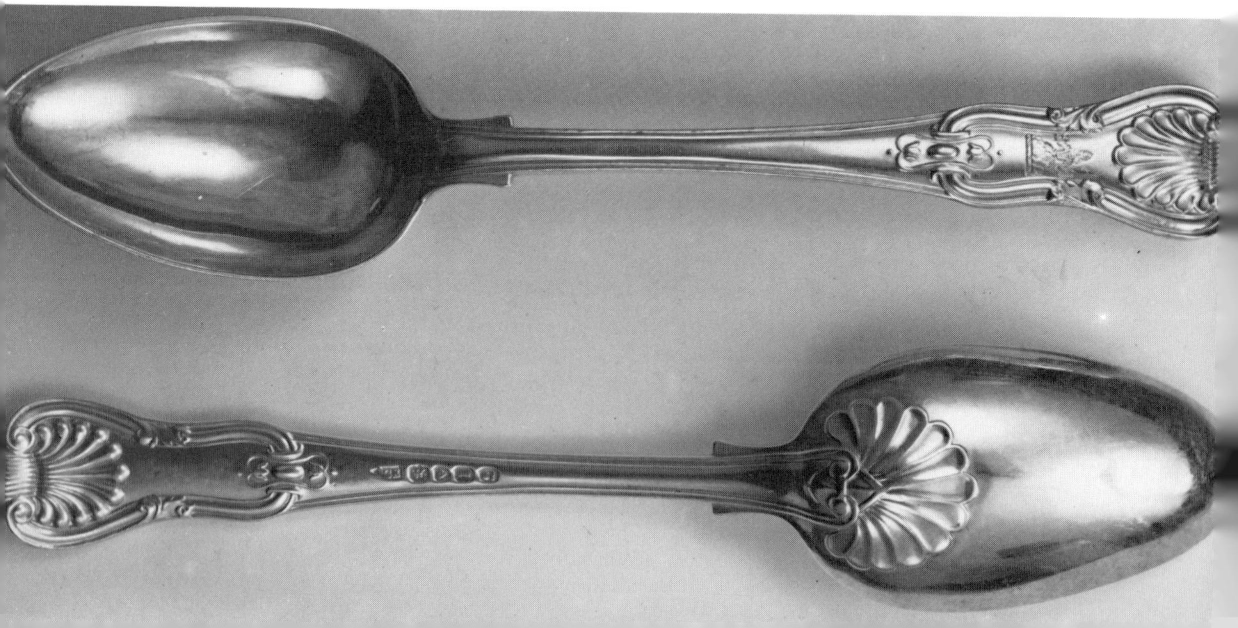

silver, were never made outside Britain. They include for instance the chased vine pattern, the Coburg pattern, the Albany pattern and the Albert pattern. At least the British spoonmakers showed that they had more imagination than their continental colleagues, though these very often invented, not new styles, but new spoon types. Many spoons for certain particular uses had been invented in the eighteenth century, but many more were produced during the nineteenth century, and one only has to read through an old nineteenth-century catalogue to realize the extent of the diversification. Manufacturers kept producing more and more table, dessert, tea, coffee, salt, mustard and olive spoons, which already existed in the preceding century, but they also produced spoons some of which have completely disappeared from the twentieth-century inventory. The best and most obvious type is the French absinthe spoon made for imbibing the French alcoholic drink made from the absinthe, a wild and toxic weed found on uncultivated ground. The making of such a killer drink was eventually forbidden by law in France, after it had killed thousands of people, and the once popular absinthe spoon ceased being produced.

Another special spoon was made for drinking maytrank, also unknown in Britain, but much more inoffensive than the absinthe, and still manufactured today. The maytrank spoon, always with a diamond-shaped bowl with pierced cover, had a variety of very long stems, some tapering flat, some of the tubular type, some in silver or other metals, others in ivory or ebony. The French made a spoon they called a 'mazagran spoon', which leaves you mystified until you learn that mazagran was nothing more than coffee, but served in a high glass—in fact the *café con leche* of the Spaniards. This spoon is similar to a dessert spoon, but has a very long stem of course. And it stopped being made a long time ago, so long in fact that everybody has now forgotten what the mazagran was.

Other spoons of nineteenth-century invention were:

Stewed fruit spoon: a spoon with a very deep outsize oval bowl with a rather long tapering stem. The spoon is too big to be a table spoon and too small to be a basting spoon.

Sauce spoon: another big spoon with a variety of stems, with an oval bowl placed sideways.

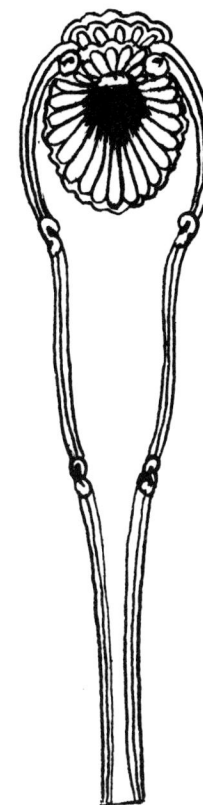

English King's Husk pattern.

123

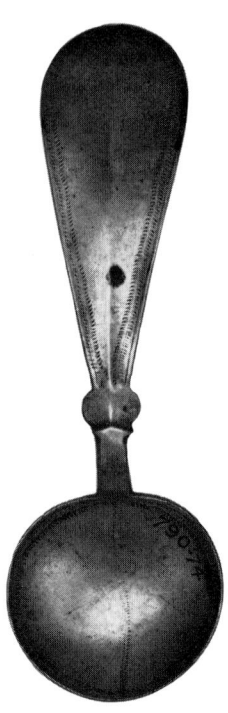

Brazilian sugar spoon: a big spoon with a deep circular bowl about 4 cm in diameter, with a long stem of the British fiddle shape type.

Strawberry spoon: a rather big spoon with a fiddle shape stem and an oval bowl placed sideways. The bowl is of course very fancy in the manner of the 'fancy front spoon' of British manufacture, with contours of various shapes.

Powdered sugar spoon: similar in size and shape to the strawberry spoon, but the bowl is always perforated.

Salad spoon: nineteenth-century salad spoons practically always have a tubular stem and a large oval bowl in various kinds of wood or in ivory.

Sweet spoon: similar in shape to the salad spoon, but somewhat smaller. It had a tubular handle, quite thick, but the bowl was of the same material as the handle, silver, silver plate or other metals.

Ice-cube spoon: newcomer to the spoon scene, it often had a fig-shaped bowl and a thin stem, of round or square section, making the spoon look older than it was. The bowl was in most cases perforated like a sugar spoon bowl. The stem was sometimes designed as a vine stock.

Olive spoon: the French olive spoon is not a nineteenth-century invention, but its production was greatly increased during the century. It has a perforated oval bowl and a long stem of the fiddle shape type.

Tuna spoon: made to serve tuna fish, and very similar to the olive spoon, but slightly smaller. It too had a perforated oval bowl, the punched holes being of various shapes, in the manner of the British mote spoon bowls. In fact it is difficult to establish the difference between an olive spoon and a tuna spoon.

Brass lustration spoon from the 19th century. *Courtesy Victoria and Albert Museum, London*

Four George III caddy spoons in silver. From left to right, a caddy spoon with a heart-shaped bowl by Joseph Wilmore, Birmingham 1804; a shovel-shaped caddy with ivory handle by Samuel Pemberton, Birmingham 1810; another shovel-shaped caddy spoon, with the initials A.D. within a tooled shield; a caddy spoon, of the so-called fiddle pattern, probably by Joseph Snatt, 1813. *Courtesy Sotheby Parke Bernet & Co., London*

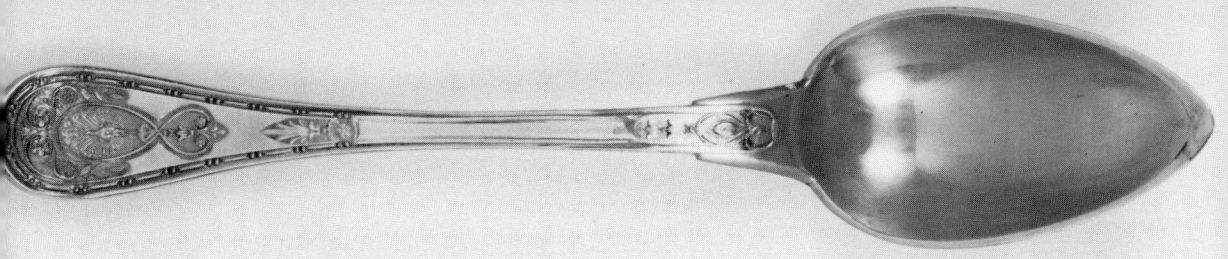

Ginger spoon: another real newcomer, this spoon is typically French and does not seem to have been made anywhere else. Research has failed to establish how it was used. It was a shovel-type spoon, the shovel itself being fiddle-shaped. Manufacturers used to sell complete ginger services comprising a ginger spoon, a cold meat fork of very unusual shape and looking like a lute when seen from above, a ginger fork with three prongs and a butter knife.

Egg spoon: two different types were made during the nineteenth century. One had an oval bowl large enough to hold an egg and with a normal type stem; the other was double-ended, with a similar bowl at one end and a very small bowl—the salt spoon—at the other.

Soda spoon: a long thin stem of round section and a very small egg-shaped bowl.

Mazagran spoon: for use with coffee served in a glass, rather similar to the soda spoon, with a long thin stem and a small ovoid bowl of slightly bigger dimension.

Beautiful example of a French Empire silver table spoon from the beginning of the 19th century.

Left: A George III caddy spoon with beaded shell-shaped bowl and 'bright-cut' handle, by William Bayley, 1786; another with similar decoration on the handle and leaf-shaped bowl, 1799; a third, plain except for the initials E.M.P. engraved on the handle, 1811; a further example, the bowl embossed with leaf motifs, probably by John Sanders, 1809; and two others, one engraved with acorns, 1809–1829. *Courtesy Sotheby Parke Bernet & Co., London*

Right: A George III caddy spoon, the oval bowl decorated with wriggle-work, possibly by R. Jewesson of Sheffield, circa 1800; another, the oval bowl set with a filigree centre, by Samuel Pemberton, 1806; a jockey cap example, modern; a fourth with pierced oval bowl, modern, Britannia Standard, all Birmingham; another, the bowl formed as a chased leaf, unmarked, circa 1810; and two Continental examples. *Courtesy Sotheby Parke Bernet & Co., London*

Water spoon: similar in general shape to the soda or mazagran spoons, with a long thin stem, often of twisted spiral shape, ending in the manner of a seal top. The seal top was used to crush the ice-cubes.

Maytrank spoon: a very strange spoon with a long and often twisted stem, the top third of which, of tubular shape, was in silver, silver plate, wood, ivory or even ebony. The bowl, diamond-shaped, had a perforated cover.

Punch spoon: like the maytrank spoon, it had a long thin stem often of twisted spiral shape, the top third of it in metal, wood or ivory. It had a diamond-shaped bowl which tapered on two sides.

Beer spoon: researches have failed to establish what these were used for, unless of course they were used to mix 'shandies' or similar mixtures of beer and other drinks. Belgians still drink a special type of beer called *gueuze*, very often mixed with syrup of grenadine. The beer spoon had a round bowl in the shape of a big daisy flower seen from above. The stem, of round or square section, had its top third in wood or ivory, of baluster shape with a ball as its finial.

Moustache spoon: very rare spoon, made, like all other spoons of nineteenth-century manufacture, in silver, silver plate or electroplate, with a guard over the side of its large bowl to protect the moustache. This spoon was made in left and right versions. It is of American origin and was patented, in 1875, by E. B. A. Mitcheson of Philadelphia. Some were produced in Britain at the end of the nineteenth century.

All those wonderful nineteenth-century spoons which could be collected can be found today in solid silver, silver plate and more often in electroplate, whose invention was the big event of the nineteenth century. If Boulsover's invention of Sheffield plate in the 1740s severely wounded the silver industry, the invention of

Beautiful Parisian silver spoon from the second half of the 19th century. Some say that such a spoon was used to eat strawberries, some say oysters. *Private collection*

French Empire silver gilt spoon and fork from the beginning of the 19th century. *Courtesy Victoria and Albert Museum*

Model 'filets' (threads) made by Christofle in 1850–1855, in silver plate. The stems are engraved with the arms of Maximilian of Mexico, who ordered them in 1865. *Bouilhel-Christofle Museum, Saint-Denis; photograph Studio Kollor, Paris*

electroplate in the 1840s dealt a final blow to the old Sheffield plate industry. The electroplate was intended to be a very cheap imitation of the already cheap Sheffield plate. It soon became very popular all over Europe, and graced all Victorian tables.

Electroplate wares are silver-plated by electrolytic deposition of a layer of silver, a very thin layer, on a base metal. The base metal most commonly used was copper, then Britannia metal and of course, but later, nickel. Elkington of Birmingham, one of the inventors of electroplate, had created his own goldmine, and he sold licences to many other flatware manufacturers, while he developed for commerce the new method of plating base metals. Yet was Elkington the inventor? When a French inventor, count de Ruolz, challenged Elkington's French patent application of 1842, a settlement was reached and honours of invention shared.

If Elkington was first in the field in Britain as the producer of flatware in electroplate, other firms were not long in following suit, such as Barker Brothers of Birmingham, and Greenbergh, who was bought later by the well-known Ellis and Company. The commonest trademark of all was the lion rampant of Barker Brothers, which can be seen on many spoons collected today. Ellis used a pineapple with trefoil clover.

Birmingham was the town where electroplated ware was first made in quantity, but Sheffield followed when Walker and Hall started production. Other firms on the Continent followed the idea, and one of the most important was none other than the Christofle concern, founded in 1830. At the beginning Charles Christofle and

his brother-in-law Joseph Bouillet made silverware, but in 1842 they bought the licence to manufacture electroplate from count de Ruolz and took him into the firm as a chemist. The electroplate wares were sold during the next ten years under the name of Ruolz. Even Christofle had troubles with his competitors and he had to file more than 300 lawsuits.

Charles Christofle began by electroplating objects which he did not produce himself, but starting in about 1850 he became supplier to the French court of Emperor Napoleon III, although before he had already supplied King Louis-Philippe. For Napoleon III he made an electroplated service of more than 1200 pieces. The firm of Christofle, which still exists today, rapidly became far the most important producer of electroplate wares in nineteenth-century France.

Germany was some way behind the British and the French. Electroplated wares were not produced by the well-known

Spoon in silver of the 'Peau de Lion' (lion's skin) pattern, made in 1870–1873 for the Marquess de Paira. *Bouilhel-Christofle Museum, Saint-Denis; photograph Studio, Paris*

Far left: The influence of plant life is again noticeable on this spoon and fork of the 1875–1880 period. The pattern 'Laurels' was produced in silver plate by Christofle. *Bouilhel-Christofle Museum, Saint-Denis; photograph Studio Kollor, Paris*
Left: The 'Shield and Garland' pattern was produced by Christofle in silver plate in 1860–1865. This spoon and fork are engraved with the arms of the notorious General Boulanger. *Bouilhel-Christofle Museum, Saint-Denis; photograph Studio Kollor, Paris*
Right: A famous Christofle pattern, 'Shield-Laurels', made in solid silver in 1860–1865. *Bouilhel-Christofle Museum, Saint-Denis; photograph Studio Kollor, Paris*
Far right: Christofle spoon and fork, of the 'Cable' pattern produced between 1845 and 1850, in silver plate. *Bouilhel-Christofle Museum, Saint-Denis; photograph Studio Kollor, Paris*

Württembergische Metallwarenfabrik until 1870. At about the same time electroplated wares were introduced into Belgium by the firm of Wiskemann S.A, which later became one of the first firms to produce stainless steel kitchen utensils, in 1924.

Two well-known firms making spoons in electroplate were the Saglier Brothers in Paris, and William Hutton and Sons in Birmingham, who made spoons in a white metal alloy (called alpacca or German silver), or nickel silver and even sometimes British plate. Alpacca is mainly used on the Continent and not in Britain. The familiar trademark of William Hutton, a group of crossed arrows, is stamped on all his articles in electroplate. James Dixon, of Birmingham, was the first to produce spoons in Britannia metal, an alloy invented before the end of the eighteenth century. Spoons in Britannia metal are always marked EPBM (Electroplated Britannia Metal). All spoons marked EPBM or EPNS (Electroplated Nickel Silver) are usually stamped with letters in separate shields which make them look like silver hallmarks. Both kinds look like silver of course, and others even look like gold. But they are not, for electrogilding was also invented around 1840, and the process was soon taken up by the Elkington firm in Birmingham.

Statistics do not exist, but it can safely be assumed that ninety per cent or more of all spoons made after 1850 or so belong to the electroplate category, not only in Britain but all over the world. Some of those spoons, always very cheap and easy to find, might be worth collecting by people who cannot afford to buy Gothic, Renaissance or even eighteenth-century silver spoons. The game would be to discover spoons made by the well-known firms such as Elkington, Ellis, Walker and Hall, Mappin and Webb, Christofle, Wiskemann and many others.

Or the collector might look for spoons which have a purpose, such as those listed above, and assemble a thematic collection of electroplate. If one can't collect expensive spoons, why not collect cheap ones? It would be very nice to own a collection of electroplated caddy spoons, strawberry spoons, ginger spoons or ice spoons, for instance, even if they only belong to the electroplate category. Collectors should however avoid electroplated spoons which are very thin and light, and spoons which are scratched. They should avoid at all cost spoons which are worn and where the

Very rare spoons of continental origin. They are beer spoons, and nobody seems to know with what kind of beer they were used for in the 19th century.

129

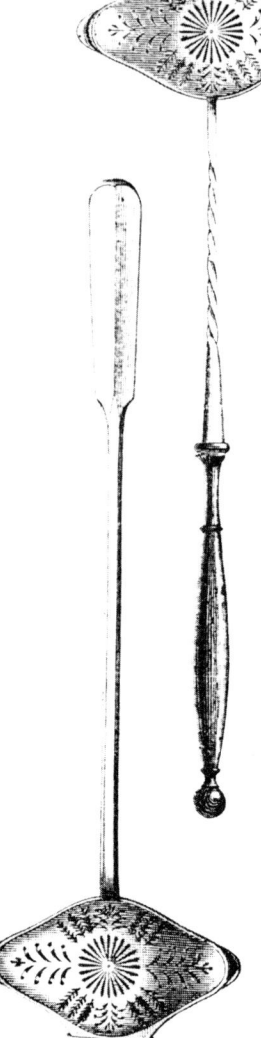

yellowish base metal shows through, and any spoons which are tarnished. Electroplated spoons were produced by the billion, and since they are practically unbreakable, a lot have survived and should not be too hard to find. As they are cheap, only the top-quality ones should be bought.

Silver spoons went on being made all through the nineteenth century, but in numbers which are insignificant when compared to the electroplated output. Most people had gone over to electroplate, even very important people like the French Emperor Napoleon III. All the spoons made in electroplate were copies of those previously made in solid silver. It is therefore quite easy to find electroplated spoons of the well-known silver patterns, for designers had still to come.

You have to wait until the very end of the nineteenth century to discover spoon manufacturers who really used their imagination or, failing that, who used the services of a real designer. The first experiments in design were tried in Britain, and at long last the inspiration came from outside Europe, this time from Japan. Elkington, the king of electroplate, experimented with champlevé and cloisonné enamelling and produced articles, including spoons, in the Japanese style shortly after 1860. A similar style was applied to silver about ten years later. In 1880, Atkin brothers of Sheffield produced salad spoons with ivory carved handles, also in the Japanese style. Europe was on its way to the Art Nouveau style, although unfortunately for spoon collectors it did not last very long—a mere fifteen years or so.

Rarer than beer spoons, the 'maytrank' spoon, with diamond shaped bowl with pierced cover. Made in 19th century France.

French silver spoon of the mid-19th century, with porcelain handle. Spoons in porcelain or with porcelain handles were made in the second half of the 18th century and in the 19th century by important porcelain factories such as Meissen, Vienna, Gournai, Chantilly, and others. *Courtesy Victoria and Albert Museum, London*

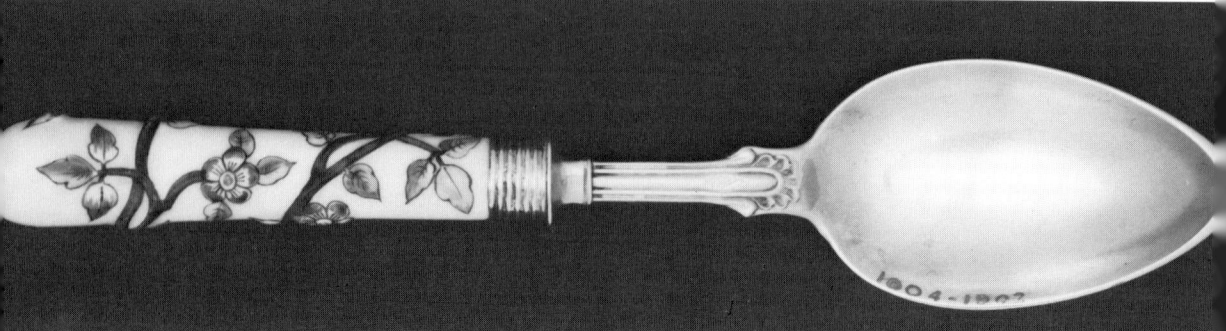

12 ART NOUVEAU SPOONS

The term Art Nouveau, which applied to the new decorative style that flourished in Europe at the turn of the century, was coined by two art-loving Belgian lawyers, Maus and Picard, who founded a magazine called *L'art Moderne* in 1881, and who as early as 1884 called themselves 'firm believers in the New Art (l'Art Nouveau)'. Samuel Bing, the Parisian art dealer, and specialist in oriental art, gave the name to his shop at the end of the year 1895. But the style went under many other names too. It was called modern style, noodle art, 1900 style and even metro style. The Germans called it 'Jugendstil', the Austrians 'Secessionsstil', and the Italians, Liberty style, after the London store. The movement started slowly during the second half of the nineteenth century, within the decorative arts, developed a certain impetus, and eventually flourished, though not really for more than ten to fifteen years. By 1910 it was practically dead.

Art Nouveau was, among other things, a reaction against imitations of earlier styles. What the artists and craftmen wanted primarily was to use a brand-new style which had nothing to do with any previous European styles. In Britain, they even urged a return to mediaeval standards of craftsmanship. It must be said that the new style so developed was only accepted by an elite, and never appealed to the man in the street. Millions of people lived through the Art Nouveau period without much noticing it.

Ornamentation in the new style used plantlife motifs in an entirely new way, and structural forms too were borrowed from nature. Flowers invaded all the arts, and Majorelle, the French furniture designer, called his productions Orchids or Waterlilies. Posters, book-bindings, glasses, vases in 'pâte de verre', furniture and ceramics were decorated with all kinds of flowers. And when the flowers would not do, the artists and craftsmen used animals and many insects, from beetles to dragonflies. Women of course inspired them all, women with flowing hair, always very serious, never smiling. Women with absent eyes, unreal, but always very graceful. The use of semi-precious stones to decorate silverware and pewterware was probably inherited from Gothic art, if not Byzantine art.

Everything was made in the new style, from buildings to door-handles. Even spoons, for craftsmen and designers did not forget them. Art Nouveau spoons could hardly be called plentiful, for their production was spread over a rather short period, but with a little bit of luck they can be found. They were made in silver, pewter, electroplate, alpacca, etc., and all types can be discovered—table spoons, dessert spoons, serving spoons and quite a lot of teaspoons also.

Four beautiful but useless silver gilt spoons, decorated with plique-à-jour enamel and made in Norway at the turn of the century. The spoon on the left, with its bowl decorated with spray and green flowers, the stem of which terminates in a spray of one green and three blue flowers, was made by Marius Hammer, of Bergen, in 1898. The other three spoons were produced by Jacob Tostrup, of Kristiana (Oslo) a few years earlier. *Courtesy Victoria and Albert Museum, London*

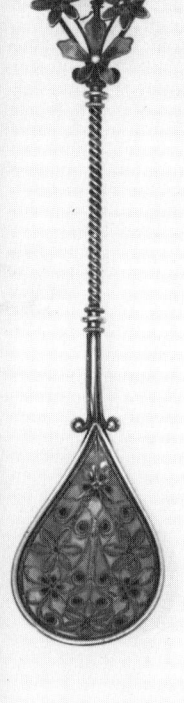

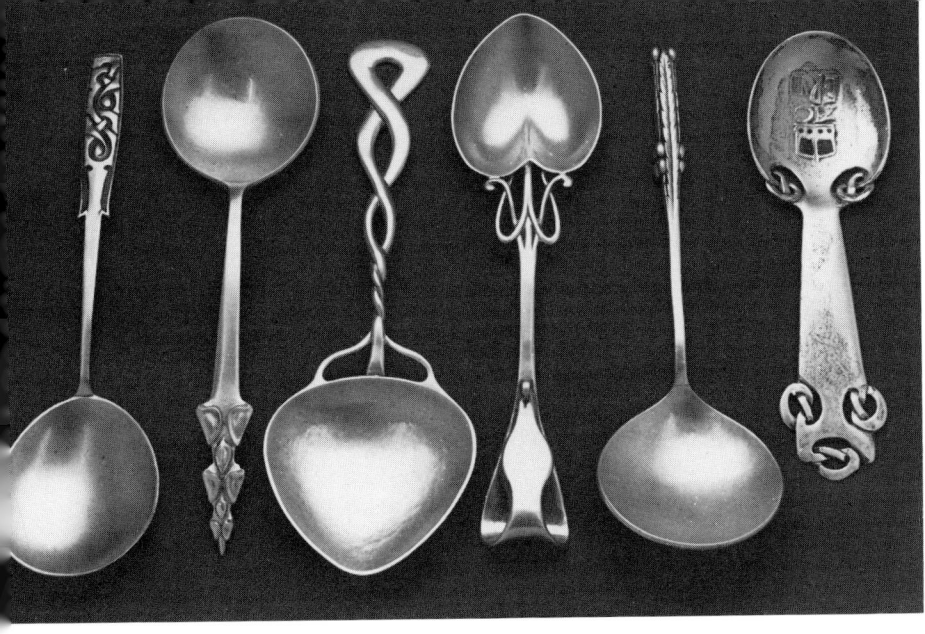

Set of six different spoons of the Cymric range by Liberty's, of London. The right hand one was made for the Coronation of Edward VIII. The two middle ones were published in 'Studio Talk': *The Studio 19* (1900) and captioned 'as designed by Oliver Baker'. They all belonged to private collections and were exhibited in the Birmingham Gold and Silver Exhibition of 1973. *Courtesy of the Birmingham Assay Office, Birmingham*

Some silver spoons were produced by great silversmiths in Britain, Germany, France and Belgium, after designs supplied by great artists, for the new style really called for designers. There was no question of copying earlier types: one had to be original or else. Some other examples were produced much more cheaply in silverplate, pewter or alpacca by industrial concerns and small tableware firms in every country where the style flourished. The general shapes did not vary much from the accepted universal types, except in a few cases when the bowls were given fancy shapes, but the stems were always decorated with the ornaments characteristic of the style, the flowers, insects, women, plants in the Japanese manner. In some rare instances they were even adorned with cabochons and enamels. (The Japanese influence did not suddenly arrive in 1895. Its infiltration had been a long process. As mentioned before, Elkington produced pieces in the Japanese style in the early 1860s, and cabinet makers made furniture inspired by Japan a few years later, giving birth to what has been called the Anglo-Japanese and Franco-Japanese styles of furniture, now extremely rare and expensive.)

It was only at the very end of the century that spoons in the Art Nouveau style started to be made. One of the great designers, Charles Rennie Mackintosh, leading exponent of the famous Glasgow school, designed tea-rooms for a Miss Cranston in Glasgow, starting in 1897.

133

Of course the remodelling of the rooms included new-style spoons. Mackintosh's spoons were in fact very simple, and did not carry the flowing decoration to be found on continental spoons. He was not as bold as his continental colleagues. The Mackintosh spoons, like his furniture, looked more akin to the Art Deco style than to Art Nouveau. Some, with oval or pear-shaped bowls, had stems similar to those of the old puritan type spoons. Others, with oval bowls, even had the old trefid finials, while still others had a very simple trefoil finial. All these spoons were manufactured in silver-plated nickel.

Another well-known Art Nouveau designer, the Belgian architect Henri van de Velde, designed spoons for the Weimar court jewellers, Hans and Willem Müller. All the van de Velde spoons were part of complete dinner services. There are serving spoons, table spoons, dessert spoons, tea and even fish spoons. Most of his bowls are oval or pear-shaped, but some are of the reverse pear-shape type, almost triangular when seen from above. The stems, although very simple in a certain way, with no decoration, are terminated in an asymmetrical curve, intended to match the curve of the palm that holds them.

A British designer, Charles Robert Ashbee, a figure in the Arts and Crafts Movement, aimed like many others to revive mediaeval craft skills. He made strange-looking spoons, one of which is illustrated in *Le Mobilier de l'Art Nouveau* by Rossana Bossaglia. This spoon, together with quite a collection of van de Velde spoons, is now in the Kunstgewerbemuseum in Zurich. The Ashbee spoons, which would have certainly amazed his mediaeval ancestors, were supposed to be

Beautiful German silver gilt serving spoon of circa 1900. *Author's collection*

Art Nouveau souvenir spoons in white metal, the stems decorated with flower motifs and insects such as the dragonfly. *Private collection*

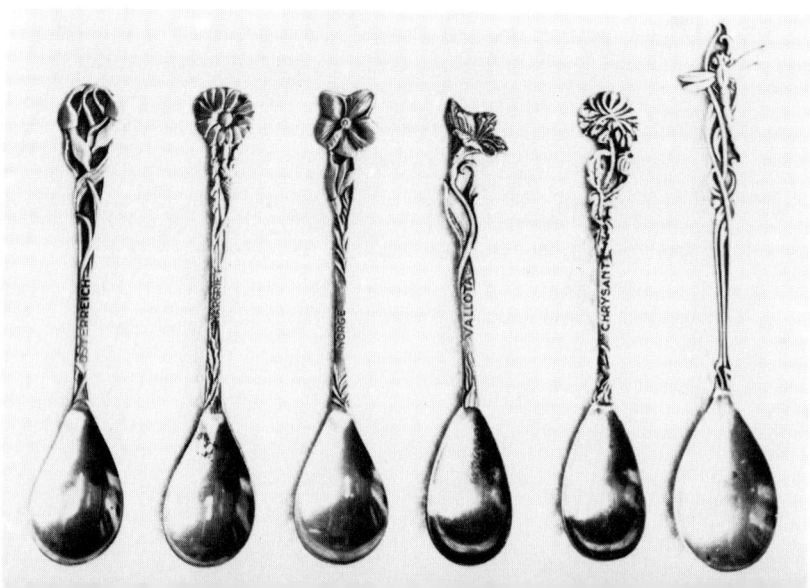

functional, but that is an open question. The stems are often bifurcated at the end, with two branches encircling a mounted turquoise cabochon before being reunited in a knot above to form the finial.

Apart from Mackintosh, Ashbee and van de Velde, some remarkable designers appeared in Germany, such as Dr Christiansen, working for the firm of P. Brückman, and Peter Behrens, who designed for Ruckert, in Mainz. Behrens was probably the more original; his spoons are of very simple design, with unusual geometric decoration on the stems. In Germany Art Nouveau was an immediate success, and many beautiful spoons were produced by German firms, mostly in silver plate or alpacca metal, although they did not always carry typical Art Nouveau ornaments. Nevertheless, although simple, they were also different: they were modern designs that had nothing to do with previous styles. Judging by the great number of spoons which survive, quite a number of German silversmiths adopted the new style. Big metalware firms like the Carl Pott concern in Sollingen produced cheap Art Nouveau spoons, although some of them, like the spoons of Mackintosh in Glasgow, already foreshadowed the succeeding style, the Art Deco of the 1920s.

At the turn of the century, when he opened his first shop, even the great Georg Jensen of Denmark realized that he had to catch attention to survive. He immediately produced flatware of what can now be seen as a typical Scandinavian design. His very first spoons were simple. They had a very normal oval bowl with a flat tapering stem ending in a slightly pointed end. The only decoration was a couple of incised bands on the stem, similar to those already found on seventeenth-century Scandinavian spoons. The pattern in its bare simplicity had such an appeal that these spoons were reproduced for a very long time. At the turn of the century the Scandinavians were already on their way, and their designers were to become famous after the First World War.

In the Britain of 1902, the Bromsgrove Guild of Applied Art produced spoons much more typical of the new Art Nouveau style, with a heart-shaped bowl and square-section stem terminated by the figure of a naked girl with flowing hair holding a mirror above her head. This type of design, with the same unusual yet beautiful stem,

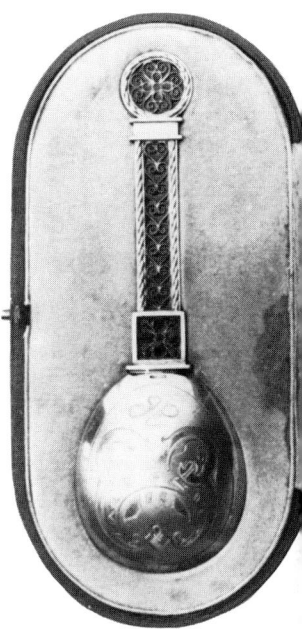

A rather extraordinary Norwegian spoon, in silver gilt, decorated with plique-à-jour enamels, by Jacob Tolstrup of Oslo, circa 1900. *Author's collection*

135

was also made in Germany, both in silver and silver gilt, still with the naked girl draped in a cloak and holding a mirror above her head, her legs twisting away to disappear into the bottom part of the stem. Who invented the pattern is a mystery: the name of the original designer is unknown, and it is difficult to determine if the design is of British or German origin. But the spoons are magnificent.

Another imaginative designer of British origin, the not so well-known Florence Stern, of Birmingham, produced some interesting spoons at the turn of the century, with ovoid bowls. The lower part of the stem is bifurcated, each branch joining the bowl by a loop. The handle is rectangular in section and is also bifurcated below the finial, which is lyre shaped, set in its centre with a tourmaline, with a silver ball as terminal. Another type made by Florence Stern has a flat stem with rectangular moulding at the top and bottom, the cast finial being formed by a bunch of three shamrocks.

Some industrial firms also made '1900 style' spoons, some in silver, but mostly in electroplate. Some extraordinary examples were made by the Christofle firm in Paris, which produced spoons of naturalistic inspiration to at last replace the much-reproduced spoons with thread and initials so beloved of nineteenth-century Frenchmen. Like many of his colleagues, Christofle thought it was time to make a break with the past. The old ornaments were replaced on the stem by asymmetrical reliefs representing leaves, onions, raspberries and even peas. Most of the Christofle spoons in electroplate are equipped with the usual ovoid bowl, with the rounded stem decorated with gilt-plated Art Nouveau motifs. Some even carry unusual decorations looking like a cigar band across the stem. Today it would be a collector's delight to discover some of the Art Nouveau spoons which Christofle made for the famous Maxim's restaurant in Paris at the turn of the century. The pattern was called 'Orchidée' because the stem of the Maxim's spoons was decorated with flowing orchids, and an orchid replaced the old drop at the junction of stem to bowl.

Of course Christofle did not suddenly hit upon the style in 1900.

One of the most beautiful and much sought after spoon and fork sets, decorated with vegetables and insects in silver gilt on a white silver background, 1875. *Bouichet-Christofle Museum, Saint-Dennis; photograph Studio Kollor, Paris*

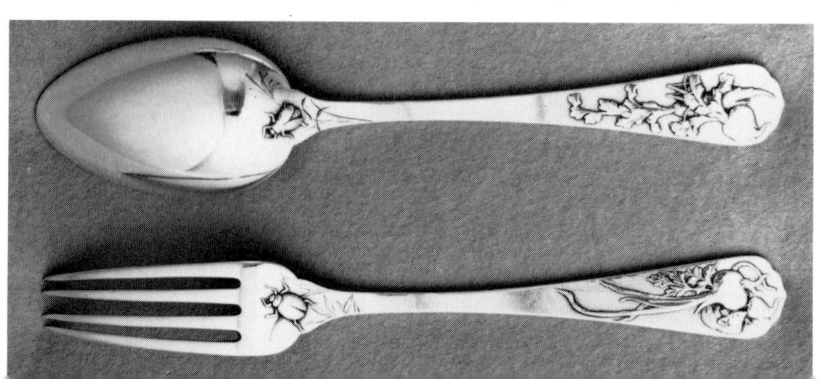

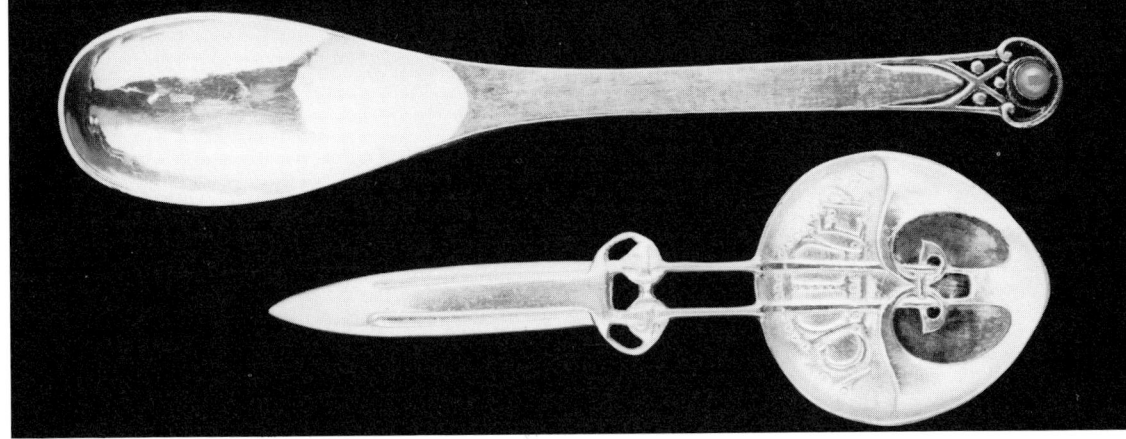

During the period 1875–80 he had already produced some magnificent spoons in which the Japanese influence was preponderant, like some in silver with gilt ornaments of flowers and vegetables, nearly always with a tiny insect in relief of the reverse of the bowl, near the junction with the stem—perhaps a little ladybird, lost at the bottom of the stem. These spoons belong to Art Nouveau, even though they were made quite a few years before the style reached its peak.

At the turn of the century, Tiffany of New York was also producing spoons, in less exuberant style than his French colleagues, more classical perhaps, but showing clear Japanese influence. Their flat stems tapered slightly, and the stem-end was cut at right-angles in the manner of the old puritan spoon pattern.

But the best chance, for British collectors at least, of picking up rare Art Nouveau spoons would be to find some of the wares sold by the Liberty retail shop in Regent Street, London, where the nicest and most unusual examples were those of the Cymric range. The Liberty shop was founded in London in the year 1875, when the Christofle shop in Paris was already making and selling his little masterpieces of craftsmanship. In 1894 Liberty too decided to make silver articles, and he registered his hallmark. Some years later he founded a new firm, Liberty and Co (Cymric) Ltd, with W. H. Haseler, silversmiths from Birmingham, as partners. Liberty was a little more restrained than his French colleagues, and he never used vegetables or flowers as decoration for his spoons, which were always of strange Celtic designs, quite different from anything else made outside Britain. Some minor designers followed the French and Belgian trend, but not Liberty.

Haseler was not the only Birmingham firm to have adopted the

Two beautiful Art Nouveau spoons of English origin. On the left, a spoon by C. R. Ashbee, in silver, decorated with a chrysoprae. On the right, a spoon by Archibald Knox, one of the Liberty designers in silver and enamel. *Courtesy John Jesse and Irina Laski, London*

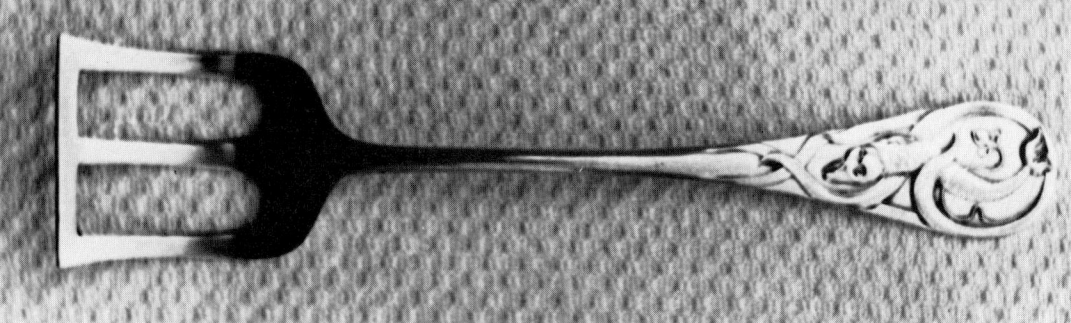

An unusual silver sardine spoon of the Art Nouveau period, the stem decorated with a sardine. The sardine spoon, made to serve sardines at the table, was a 19th-century invention. Probably German. *Author's collection*

Celtic (or Cymric) designs. William Hutton and Sons Ltd, of Sheffield and Birmingham, who became a leading Art Nouveau producer in Britain, also supplied Liberty with spoons. But Hutton, like his colleague Haseler, did not only sell spoons of the Cymric range to Liberty; he also sold them under his own name, with his own hallmark on them. Those supplied to Liberty were stamped of course with the Liberty hallmark registered in Birmingham in 1901. Some of the Cymric range spoons by Liberty's were included in 1973 in an exhibition to celebrate the bicentenary of the Birmingham Assay Office. The catalogue of the exhibition contains some very detailed descriptions of these spoons, all in silver of course. As early as 1898, Liberty made spoons with a plain circular bowl not attached but flowing practically into a straight square section stem terminating in a cast decoration of leaves and berries. In 1900 he made other spoons with a heart-shaped bowl, a very unusual but definitely not a very practical shape, with a cruciform stem, the arms joining the bowl on two sides.

Liberty also sold some very rare and interesting spoons to celebrate the coronation of Edward VII. At least three different types were produced. One had the heart-shaped type of bowl, with the simple decoration of a royal crown and two egg-shaped patches of blue enamel inscribed AC/ER VII. The second type of coronation spoon had a shield-shaped bowl inscribed Anno/Coron/ERVII. The third type, also made in 1901, had a less elaborate bowl, oval with a broad flat stem with pierced strapwork. The bowl is also inscribed AC/ERVII. These spoons, which were never again reproduced, are of course easy to identify.

Starting in 1902 and until well into the 1920s, Liberty made yet another type of Cymric spoon, which should be easy to find since its output was spread over a couple of decades. This spoon also had a heart-shaped bowl, with a central spine, the stem being joined to the bowl by an ornament spreading as tendrils over the back of the bowl from the central stalk of the stem.

Liberty has the reputation of not publicizing his designers, but we know that the coronation spoons, for instance, were designed by Oliver Baker, and that another well-known designer, A. Knox, from the Isle of Man, was also responsible for some of the spoons. Apart from those mentioned above, other spoons of the Cymric range were produced by Liberty, some of them from 1902 into the 1920s, so quite a number of them must still be around today. Some were

Silver forks, knives and spoons, designed by Art Nouveau architect Henri Van de Velde in 1906. *Copyright A.C.L., Brussels*

decorated with semi-precious stones like turquoise, or with enamels of various colours.

Liberty, yet again Liberty, launched another type of article in 1902. The Tudric range was very similar in style to the silver articles of the Cymric range, only in pewter this time. And the spoons of the Tudric range, as striking to look at as those from the Cymric range, are always stamped with the mark L & Co. The Tudric spoons are also marked 'Tudric pewter' followed by the stock number of the piece. The association between Liberty and Haseler ceased in 1926, and that was the end of the marvellous spoons of the two ranges.

Another beautiful type of spoon was made in Norway, and it too is linked with Liberty of London. Some Norwegian silversmiths had the bright idea a few years before the turn of the century of using enamels to decorate their silverware, and they made beautiful and very fragile spoons decorated with plique à jour enamels of various colours. Apparently the first silversmith to do so was Jacob Tostrup, of Oslo, who was soon followed by one of his colleagues in the town, David Andersen. Similar spoons were also made by the silversmith Marius Hammer, of Bergen, on the west coast of Norway.

These spoons, which are in fact useless, were probably intended for the tourist market or to be sold as souvenirs, for nobody could use them to eat. They are as fragile as glass. They were marketed in Britain by Liberty, and several are illustrated in his catalogue of

Typical of the Art Nouveau style, this spoon of the 'Orchid' pattern, was produced by Christofle at the end of the 19th century, exclusively for 'Maxim's', the famous Paris restaurant. *Bouilhel-Christofle Museum, Saint-Denis; photograph Studio Kollor, Paris*

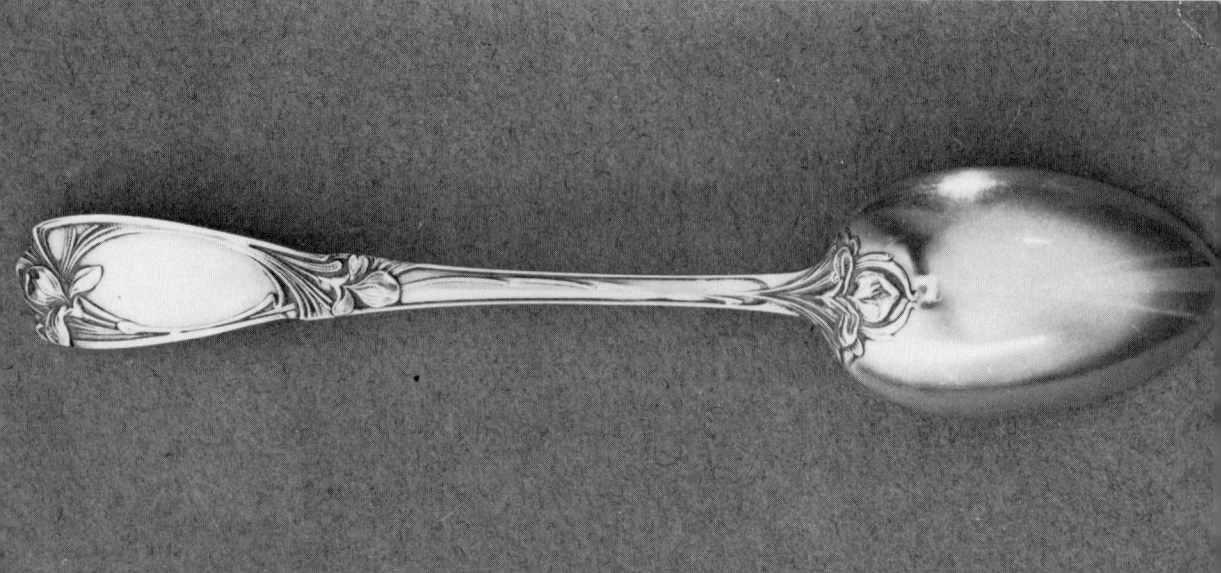

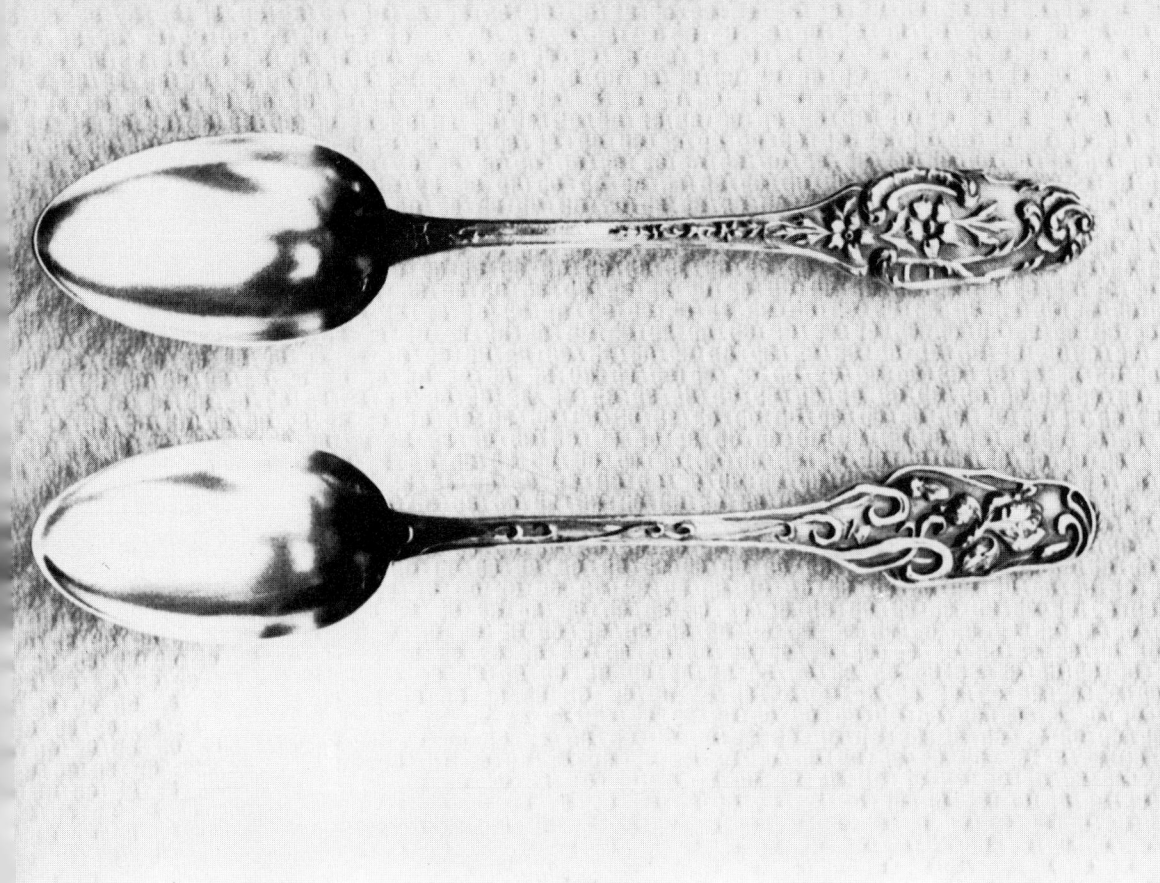

Two different Belgian silver spoons of the Art Nouveau period. *Author's collection*

1895–6, where they are advertised at 18s 6d each, quite a large sum for the time. Today the price would be around £100–£150. At Christmas in 1899, Liberty stocked a whole range of enamelled Norwegian spoons, sold singly or in boxes of six. Of course he was not the only one in the world to sell enamelled spoons by the three Norwegian silversmiths at the turn of the century, as these spoons were exported to many countries. They can therefore be found practically anywhere, and one was sold lately on the Brussels flea market for the equivalent of £50 to a lucky collector. Quite a lot of them are now in museums, and the best place to see some of them is the Victoria and Albert in London.

The very delicate Norwegian silver spoons, whose production spans about two decades, are hard to describe because they are all different, with different types of bowl, different stems and different enamels. Some bowls are oval, others circular, others pear-shaped. The stems and bowls are always decorated with stylized flowers in enamel in various shades of blue, green and red, often with yellow centres. The spoons are not always marked, as there was not enough room to stamp a hallmark on them, so one has to know them to recognize them. When only the stems are enamelled, a hallmark consisting of the initials of the marker is stamped on the reverse of the bowl. The Norwegian silversmiths who made these little enamelled masterpieces were not as shy as Liberty's when it came to disclosing the names of the designers, and Norwegian authors mention that Gustav Gauderneck was the designer for Andersen and Rorolf Prytz for Tostrup.

Judging by their relative abundance in sales rooms, antique shops and, as mentioned above, in flea markets, millions of Art Nouveau spoons of all types and in all kinds of metals were made both by the big flatware firms and by small concerns, some of them in silver, but mostly in electroplate or other white alloys. A sizeable collection could still be assembled without undue difficulty, each one a little masterpiece, pleasant to look at and to handle, reminders of a short-lived style which rose and fell in the space of less than two decades.

SELECTIVE BIBLIOGRAPHY

Henri d'Allemagne *Less Accessoires du costume et de la décoration*, Paris

Germain Bapst, *Etudes sur l'étain*, Paris 1884

Berndorff, catalogue published in Austria in 1902

Birmingham Gold and Silver 1773–1973, catalogue of exhibition, Birmingham 1973

Rossana Bossaglia *Le Mobilier de l'Art Nouveau*, Paris 1972
Paris 1972

P. H. Boucaud and Claude Fregnac *Les Etains*, Fribourg 1978

Rev. Dom Fernand Cabron and RP Dom Henry Leclercq *Dictionnaire d'archéologie chrétienne et de liturgie*, Paris 1914

Catalogue of Scandinavian and Baltic Silver, Victoria and Albert Museum, 1975

Christofle, catalogue published in France in 1883

Michael Clayton *Silver and Gold of Great Britain and North America*, New York 1971

Henri Clouzot *Les Arts due Métal*, Paris 1934

The Complete Encyclopedia of Antiques, The Connoisseur, London 1962

O. M. Dalton *Catalogue of Early Christian Antiquities in the British Museum*, London 1901

Daremberg and Saglio *Dictionnaire des antiquités grecques et romaines*, Paris 1887

Dictionnaire universel francois et latin, Paris 1771

A. Fochier-Henrion *Les Etains populaires de France*, Paris 1968

Victor Gay *Glossaire d'archéologie du Moyen-Age et de la Renaissance*, Paris 1887

Grand dictionnaire Larousse du XIXième siècle, Paris

Henry Harvard *Dictionnaire de l'ameublement et de la décoration*, Paris

Carl Hernmarck *The Art of the European Silversmiths 1430–1830*, London 1977

Graham Hughes *Modern Silver*, London 1967

D. van der Kellen *Nederlands Oudheden*, Amsterdam 1861

E. M. Ch. F. Klijn *Oude zilveren lepels*, Lochem 1967

Oxford Companion to the Decorative Arts, 1975

L. Pissarkaia, N. Platonova and B. Ulianova *Russkie Emali XI–XIX BB*, Moscow 1974

M. M. Postnikova-Loseva, H. G. Platonova and B. L. Ulbanova *Russkoe Tsernevoe Iskusstvo*, Moscow 1972

Adolphe Riff *Etains strasbourgeois du XVIième au XIXième siècle*, Strasbourg 1925

Russkoe Houdojestvennoe Serebro, catalogue of silver wares in the Hermitage Museum, Leningrad 1877

Eric J. G. Smith 'The English Silver Spoon' Parts 1 to 4, published in *Antique Dealer and Collector's Guide*, London